PRAISE FOR THE I

M000206019

"Finley successfully connects weaving a meaningful tapestry of symbolism, stories, sacraments, and more—convincing even the most tired of moms that moments of redemption abound in their days."

—Therese J. Borchard, mother of two, editor of *I Love Being a Mom: Treasured Stories, Memories, and Milestones*

"As a mother, I know the yearning of my maternal spirit for greater connection to Mother Church.
This book offers insight into that mystical union and elevates the ordinary rituals of our family life.
As founder of Elizabeth Ministry, this book is an answer to prayers. I have listened to thousands of mothers seeking validation for the spirituality of facing the joys, challenges and sorrows of childbearing and rearing. Kathleen has captured the essence of all that it means to be mother!"

—Jeannie Hannemann, M.A., mother of two young adults and founder of Elizabeth Ministry International

"What a gift! A book that affirms the sacredness of all those moments, experiences, and feelings that are absolutely core to mothers' lives. I felt acknowledged, lifted up, renewed and inspired."

—Kathy McGinnis, mother of three adopted children, grandmother of two, executive director of the Institute for Peace and Justice

THE LITURGY OF MOTHERHOOD

Also by Kathleen Finley

Dear God: Prayers for Families with Children
Our Family Book of Days: A Record through the Years
The Seeker's Guide to Building a Christian Marriage: 11 Essential Skills
Savoring God: Praying with All Our Senses
Welcome: Prayers for New and Pregnant Parents

Coauthored with husband Mitch Finley

Building Christian Families
The People's Catechism

THE LITURGY
OF MOTHERHOOD

Moments of Grace

Kathleen Finley

SHEED & WARD
Lanham • Chicago • New York • Toronto • Oxford

Published by Sheed & Ward
An Imprint of Rowman & Littlefield Publishers, Inc.
A wholly owned subsidiary of The Rowman & Littlefield Publishing Group, Inc.
4501 Forbes Boulevard, Suite 200
Lanham, MD 20706

PO Box 317
Oxford
OX2 9RU, UK

Distributed by National Book Network

Library of Congress Cataloging-in-Publication Data

Finley, Kathy.
    The liturgy of motherhood : moments of grace / Kathleen Finley.
        p. cm.
    Includes bibliographical references.
    ISBN 1-58051-145-7 (hardcover : alk. paper)—ISBN 1-58051-113-9 (pbk. : alk.
paper)
    1. Motherhood—Religious aspects—Christianity. I. Title.
BV4529.18.F56 2004
248.8'431—dc22

Printed in the United States of America.

♾™ The paper used in this publication meets the minimum requirements of
American National Standard for Information Sciences—Permanence of
Paper for Printed Library Materials, ANSI/NISO Z39.48-1992.

CONTENTS

Introduction

MOTHERHOOD AND LITURGY: WHAT'S THE CONNECTION?

A MOTHER COMFORTS HER CHILD AND PUTS THE LITTLE one to her breast to nurse; a eucharistic minister distributes the host to those coming up for communion at Mass. Completely different actions—or could they be linked in some way? And if liturgy and motherhood *are* connected, could those connections provide a lens by which to explore the spirituality of mothers?

Before exploring any common ground between the two, we need to first clarify the term "liturgy." The *HarperCollins Encyclopedia of Catholicism* briefly defines liturgy as "the public and official rites of the Church." The *American Heritage Dictionary* describes it as the rite of the Eucharist or as a prescribed form for a public religious service, a ritual. The word "liturgy" originally comes from the Greek for "the work of the people," something done not only *by* the people but also *for* the common good. Through the many centuries of the Christian church, liturgy has developed in both the West and the East as a set of rituals that celebrate the mysteries of the life of faith and as a calendar of feasts and seasons of the Christian life.

With this basic sense of what liturgy is and an awareness of the experience of motherhood, we can now ask what liturgy and motherhood have in common.

At first glance, there would seem to be many more differences than similarities. How can there be much of an intersection between the two when motherhood seems to be rather private and happens mainly at home, while liturgy is quite public and occurs in church? Motherhood concerns women, while liturgy usually involves men in leadership roles—especially in the Roman Catholic tradition. Motherhood can be rather informal and even lighthearted at times, while liturgy seems formal and quite serious.

But when we begin to look for common elements between the two, the experience of ritual comes quickly to mind. While the first meaning in the *American Heritage Dictionary* for "ritual" is that of a prescribed form or order of conducting a religious or solemn ceremony, one of the other meanings listed is a detailed method or procedure faithfully or regularly followed. And even the example given to illustrate this meaning comes right from a mom's experience: "Her household chores have become a ritual with her."

Indeed, rituals *do* abound in the life of a mother, from naptime to baths to meals to bedtime and much that is in between. The rites of motherhood may not look as formal as liturgical rituals, but woe to the babysitter who doesn't know the right bedtime routine when dealing with a three or four year old; the new sitter will quickly be informed about the way it's done!

Besides the notion of ritual, many other links between liturgy and motherhood begin to suggest themselves on closer examination.

Both motherhood and liturgy are about the depth of human experience; they occur in a particular time but express and nurture a timeless and inexpressible reality, a relationship of love. This relationship goes so far beyond words, in both cases, that ritual actions and symbols are the only ways to try to express what can't be fully said. And, therefore, both are enacted and celebrated over and over and are never finished.

Both liturgy and motherhood also have many variations as to how this relationship of love is expressed in different times and places—as well as some common themes, as we will see throughout this book.

Both are intensely personal and private realities, and at the same time they are also communal and public. (Unfortunately, in our highly individualistic culture the communal aspect of both these experiences is frequently discounted and underappreciated.)

Both are built on the support of a wider community—whether church or family—and both celebrate life and allow more life-giving energy to flow from the experience.

Both experiences involve various senses—music, actions, smells, and words—through hymns as well as lullabies; blessings as well as rocking, feeding, and holding; incense as well as baby powder and cooking odors; scripture as well as stories and words of love and discipline.

And yet both involve a contemplative presence, where much more may be "said" and "accomplished" by silence at times than by any elaborate words or actions.

Both have a differentiation of roles—that of mother and presider as distinct from that of child and congregation or assembly—but in fact, there may be less separation of roles in both than it may appear. In the liturgy, as the Second Vatican Council reminded us, the *whole community* is really offering worship, and although it is the mother who seems to be doing all the nurturing, she will often find that there is a certain sense in which *she* is also being nourished as she cares for her child.

The focus of both motherhood and liturgy is communion, connection, and a reaffirming of the link, the relationship

3

of love. And, when seen in faith, both involve not merely human actions but also nothing less than the actions of the mystical body of Christ at work in the world, dying and rising in a continuous process.

ABOUT THIS BOOK

Using the liturgical year as our framework, we will explore the spirituality of many kinds of mothers and the ways that various aspects of the Catholic Christian tradition—such as the sacraments and the spiritual and corporal works of mercy—may be helpful in seeing more clearly the holiness of a mother's role.

Within each liturgical season, we will first explore what that season is and some particular themes of the season, along with seeing how several related practices from the Christian tradition apply to mothers' experience. We will then examine a particular quality of the spirituality of mothers as it relates to that season; before we're done we will have seen how mothers' spirituality is communal, incarnational, nurturing, compassionate and patient, wondering and imaginative, and emotionally integrated. And, because any quality can be unhealthy when it isn't balanced well in our lives, we will probe how each quality of mothers' spirituality might be less than healthy at times when it is out of balance.

We'll also examine one or two of the seven Catholic sacraments for each season and its implications in mothers' experiences. And we'll hear comments from mothers as they relate to the themes of each season, thanks to women whom I asked to share their reflections on the experience of motherhood. And, because the many women from our faith tradition can be a rich resource, we will briefly explore in each season several saints or models from scripture and Christian life for moms, and we'll also consider some scripture passages on which it may be helpful to reflect—alone or with a group of other mothers—in relation to that particular theme and season. Finally, there will be some reflection questions for each season and suggestions for further resources that you may find helpful.

Our lives as mothers are so busy that you may end up picking up and putting down this book quite often; hopefully, reading just a section at a time will still be helpful and may be all that is possible for you. *Please note*: you don't need to wait until a particular season to read that section; the liturgical year merely gives us a framework to look at the spirituality of mothers, to see the broad, multicolored—and multilayered—quilt of mothers' faiths and lives spread out before us.

As we "unroll" this rich quilt of the liturgy of motherhood, one of the key aspects of the "design" that we will see is as old as the Christian church: the tradition of families as the *domestic church*. From the time of the early Christian communities until now, the first place that Christians have gathered to share their faith is in their homes. This foundational way of gathering Christians for what we call "church" was rediscovered with the Second Vatican Council, but it can still be too easily overlooked in an era when we first think of the larger institution when we hear the term "church."

A few disclaimers may also be in order here. First, while this book will use Catholic terminology and will draw on the riches of the Catholic tradition, it is meant for all Christians and for others who may find the connections suggested here to be helpful. And in suggesting the links between Catholic practices and mothers' everyday experience, the goal is certainly not to trivialize the faith, but the opposite: to show its connection to daily life more fully.

Second, much of what will be described here as what mothers do is also what fathers and others do; the comments are not meant to be prescriptive or limiting but, rather, to be *descriptive* of many mothers' experience.

Third, I have tried to avoid being romantic and overly sentimental about mothers and motherhood; indeed, there are few areas of human experience that are easier to idealize. However, any mom who has "been there" will tell you that being a mom is "hazardous duty" a good deal of the time, and that none of us do anywhere near a perfect job at it. In fact, some mothers are *not* able to do a healthy job of caring for their children, although—thankfully—those mothers are in the minority.

Whether severely wounded or just slightly so, mothers have the potential to be the first sacrament—a tangible, visible sign of God's intangible, invisible love—in the lives of their children; it is that reality that we want to explore more fully here.

A Note about the Liturgical Year

There are two major cycles in the liturgical year for Christians: the **Easter cycle**, which includes Lent, Holy Week, and Easter through until Pentecost, and the **Christmas cycle**, running from Advent through Christmas to Epiphany. Sundays that fall outside these cycles—from Epiphany to Ash Wednesday and Pentecost until the beginning of Advent—are referred to as **Ordinary Time**. This latter term is not because this time is less special but because most Sundays in this season are referred to by their *order*: for example, the Sixteenth Sunday in Ordinary Time.

In order to discover how these times of the year may help us explore mothers' experience, we will expand these cycles into their various seasons: Advent, Christmas/Epiphany, Lent, Holy Week/Easter, Pentecost, and Ordinary Time.

Chapter One

ADVENT
Waiting in Hope

As SHE WAITED FOR HER DAUGHTER TO COME HOME FROM the dance, Mona found herself remembering all the other times throughout her life that she had ended up waiting for Emily—all the way back to anticipating becoming pregnant with her, carrying her for what seemed like an endless nine months of pregnancy before her birth, and even going through twelve hours of labor with her, hours that seemed like they would never end. Then another kind of waiting began; there was anticipating her first smile and her learning to crawl, watching her learn to walk and listening for her first words, and finally waiting for her to be potty trained.

Although the time since then had seemed to fly—even more so since Seth, Emily's younger brother, was born—there were still plenty of times spent waiting: for Emily to realize that doing a major project the night before it was due was not wise, for example, or waiting with her to find out whether she made the team or the cast of the play. Would she ever, Mona wondered, stop waiting for *something* in her life as a mom?

WHAT IS THIS SEASON?

Just as waiting, in one way or another, seems to permeate the experience of mothers, it is also a key part of the liturgical season of Advent. Late November or early December can seem like a strange time of year to begin a calendar, but the church year starts with a time of preparation, of waiting and longing for the celebration of the birth of Jesus at Christmas. At the darkest—and what can seem like the deadest—time of the year, at least in the Northern Hemisphere, we long for Light and Life.

The four weeks of Advent (from the Latin word for "coming") are a time to anticipate the coming, not only of the infant Jesus at Christmas, but also, as the liturgy puts it, to "wait in joyful hope for the coming of our Savior, Jesus Christ" in glory at the end of time. Not only are both these themes present in the readings for the season, there is also another tension very evident at this time of year. *Waiting* for Jesus can seem almost impossible, especially with children, when the culture around us has already *begun* the Christmas season right after Halloween and keeps singing about someone else coming to town!

But this crunch between faith and culture may have always been there, in one form or another, even for the early Christians. We don't have any accurate way of knowing at what time of year Jesus was actually born; it doesn't seem to have been important enough for the first Christians to record. The dating of Christmas, and, therefore, Advent, was in place by the fourth century; however, and some experts think that it was planned to coincide with the pagan celebration of the unconquered sun at the winter solstice, when the days are shortest and nights are longest. And just preceding that was the five-day harvest festival of Saturnalia, beginning on December

17, a time of gift giving and feasting and excesses. (Sound familiar?) To counteract this, church officials tried to emphasize a more somber tone, with some fasting and longing expressed in such prayers as the "O Antiphons," (see below.) So the feast of Christmas and the season of Advent have had some sort of "competition" since the very beginning.

What does this season of waiting and preparation have to say to mothers today? Plenty, as Gertrud Mueller Nelson suggests in *To Dance with God*:

> Our masculine world wants to blast away waiting from our lives. Instant gratification has become our constitutional right and delay an aberration. We equate waiting with wasting. . . . [But] as in a pregnancy, nothing of value comes into being without a period of quiet incubation: not a healthy baby, not a loving relationship, not a reconciliation, a new understanding, a work of art, never a transformation. Rather, a shortened period of incubation brings forth what is not whole or strong or even alive. Brewing, baking, simmering, fermenting, ripening, germinating, gestating are the feminine processes of becoming and they are the symbolic states of being which belong in a life of value, necessary to transformation. (p. 62)

One of these slow processes in our lives is the gradual discovery that, in a sense, we are called to be like Mary. Although not in the literal sense that was true for her, *all* Christians are called to carry and give birth to Christ, to bear the Word to those around them. How each of us will do that is as unique as the gifts God has given us, but it is what we are called to do, and it may well take us a lifetime to fully understand what that means.

Advent and waiting have much indeed to teach us about listening more deeply to ourselves and to our experience and seeing the ways God is at work in the midst of all of it.

FROM THE TRADITION

What practices from the Christian tradition can help enhance our appreciation of the season of Advent and of waiting in our lives? One is the **Advent wreath**, a custom that began among sixteenth-century German Lutherans and has spread to many Christians, but which probably has pagan roots because we know that most cultures had a festival of lights at the darkest time of the year.

Around the wreath, which is usually lying flat and covered with evergreens, are four candles, one for each Sunday of the season. Three of the candles are usually purple and one is pink—for the third Sunday of Advent, which has a more joyful theme and is called Gaudete Sunday. Gaudete is Latin for "Rejoice," which is the first word of the opening prayer for this Sunday, because the feast of Christmas is drawing closer.

Especially when other lights in the house are turned off, we can see week after week, as we pray around the wreath, a dramatic sense of the light overcoming the darkness as we go from one candle in the dark to four in the last week before Christmas.

The Advent wreath reminds us that our lives hold both light *and* darkness, both hope *and* fear; that reality hasn't changed with the "advent" of electric sources of light. Mothers wonder: should we push our children a bit more? Are we pushing too hard? Will they be safe? Should we give them more freedom? How do we share our faith with them? We still worry and question, *and* we still experience our faith as a light that helps dispel that darkness.

Another Advent tradition comes from the Latin American culture. **Las Posadas** (Spanish for "the inns") is a traditional Hispanic festival that reenacts Mary and Joseph's search for room at the inn. Each Christmas season, a procession accompanies two people dressed as Joseph and Mary, who walk through the community streets. The processional stops at a previously selected home and the couple asks for lodging for the night. The people are invited in to read scriptures and sing Christmas carols called "alguinaldos." Refreshments are provided by the hosts. This continues for eight nights in commemoration of the journey of Mary and Joseph from Nazareth to Bethlehem.

Just as Mary and Joseph found no room in the inn, sometimes even when mothers have a comfortable home and a "good" family, they can feel like there isn't any place where they are fully accepted or understood. For example, no one quite understands the unique way mothers both deeply love their children and yet also need to keep growing as individuals and women, apart from their children. Mothers need to remember that the only real "place" where they are fully loved, fully accepted, and welcomed is in God's love, a God who knows well our fears and our feelings of not being fully received and appreciated at times.

The **O Antiphons** are the prayers of longing that now form the Alleluia verses for the Masses from December 17 to 23; we know them best as the verses to the carol "O Come, O Come, Emmanuel." They are a mosaic of biblical verses from both prophetic and wisdom books and probably date from the seventh or eighth centuries. They begin on the first day with the invitation, "O wisdom, Holy word of God, you reach from one end of the earth to the other with providential and tender care. Come and teach us to live in your ways," and end with "O Emmanuel, Giver of a new law to all nations, come and save us for you are our God."

Along with the O Antiphons, mothers also cry at times, "Come, God of love, and help us with our families, with these relationships, help us to see how you are present in the midst of what can seem too chaotic and too ordinary to be holy; help us to see you both in the darkness and in the glimpses of light."

MOTHERS' SPIRITUALITY IS *COMMUNAL*

As we wait for Jesus' coming in our lives, as Mary did, women often do the first thing that scripture tells us Mary did as she was coping with what was, in a sense, a "problem pregnancy." After finding out that she was to give birth to the Savior, she went to see another woman.

"During those days Mary set out and traveled to the hill country in haste to a town of Judah, where she entered the house of Zechariah and greeted Elizabeth" (Luke 1:39–40). Here Mary and Elizabeth show us a delight in each other and a sharing and support as complementary equals which is rarely found elsewhere in scripture.

As mothers we tend to be communal rather than individualistic, or even hierarchical, in how we approach our lives and our spirituality. This goes back as far as women gathering at the well to share both their wisdom and their concerns; our support for one another as women is a strong resource for each of us. Feminist writer Judith Plaskow calls this sharing of women's consciousness the "yeah, yeah experience."

Mothers know intuitively that each of us is a network of relationships and that we come to God together or not at all. This *web of relationships* for each person includes all those who have helped shape that person: siblings, parents, a spouse (if married), and children. These are bonds that have shaped us indelibly and through which we have also helped shape others' lives. Very few of these relationships are ones that we choose—apart from a spouse or a good friend—but in faith we know that *God* has chosen just these people to help us build the basis for our faith. This is where we learn about love—and about joy, hope, and even about forgiveness, since none of these people—including us—is perfect.

We celebrate this web of relationships in powerful ways both at home and in church. Whenever we celebrate birthdays, we ritualize not only the goodness and gift of the birthday person but also the importance of the relationships we have with that person. And in the liturgy of the Eucharist, just after the Lord's Prayer, we are reminded of the communal dimension to our faith and ritualize it as we extend to those around us the sign of peace, sharing the consolation and love that Jesus offers us with one another.

These simple actions are in contrast to many of the ways our culture sees what it means to be a full person. Those who study human development have so far focused on the process—and, rather, male pattern—of *separation and achievement* in reaching adulthood, while women seem to instead focus on *relationships and interdependence,* topics that are finally beginning to be studied by researchers such as Carol Gilligan.

Women find support from one another in many ways, and this communal quality to mothers' spirituality affects everything we do, including how we communicate. Those who study women's communication say that we are focused on connection—on the *how* rather than the *what* of communication—that we like to talk more than men, especially at home, and that we usually talk face-to-face, rather than side-by-side, which is more typical for men. Men often find the amount of talking women do to be puzzling; for women it's the way we connect with others.

As women carry that strong sense of "we" rather than "I" into their spirituality, they are often quite open to sharing their spirituality with others, and they bring this network of relationships with them as they come to God in prayer. Mothers have a sense of the **communion of saints**—the connection between all believers, even beyond the grave—that is intuitive; we know it's not just "me and God." (The two main feasts celebrating the communion of saints happen in early November, a few weeks before Advent begins: the feast of All Saints on November 1 and All Souls on November 2.)

ACHIEVING A BALANCE

When it comes to the communal nature of their faith, mothers can tend, on the one hand, to be *too concerned about others*, especially about their concerns and problems, and not step back to see the ways in which *God is at work* in the lives of those they love. Mary and Elizabeth both cared deeply for one another, but they also knew that what was happening to them was *not about them*, but what God was doing in their lives. They both also found themselves in unusual pregnancies, in situations where they could easily have been worried about what others might think of them.

When mothers don't respect proper boundaries with others or realize the importance of charity, what can easily result is gossip—loose or irresponsible talk about someone else to a third party. It is interesting to note that the word "gossip" originally comes from a term for a godparent, a *god-sib*, but evidently deteriorated to what we know today, just as the communal aspect of our spirituality can deteriorate when it gets out of balance.

On the other hand, moms can also *fail to be aware of and open to others* around them because, paradoxically, they are often not honoring their own needs enough to let others be who they are. An example here might be the mother who has a tough time supporting a young adult son who is question-ing his faith—because she has not really faced *her own* ques-tions about God.

More and more mothers and women seem to be gath-ering together in groups to share their faith with one an-other, and they are finding that important energies are unleashed when they do so. Mothers know if that if they lis-ten well to what is happening through them and in their lives, they will see that the source of what they discover there is *God*, not themselves, and they will understand better how to love others—without gossip—and how to allow them-selves to be loved in turn.

PREGNANCY: NOW IT BEGINS

What experiences of mothers does the season of Advent invite us to explore? One natural topic is that of pregnancy, as we cel-ebrate the end of Mary's pregnancy. Most women who have been pregnant remember well watching their bellies—some-how, pregnant women no longer seem to have stomachs but bellies instead—grow and, perhaps, even their navels change. It can be hard to tell if the first few kicks are really there or just a fluttery feeling inside. The initial uncertainty about whether or not they were really pregnant has already been confirmed by a positive pregnancy test and, later, by hearing the amazing heartbeat from within. And then the waiting and preparing be-gins—sometimes anxiously and sometimes calmly.

When I was pregnant with our oldest son, my husband and I had just moved into our first house, an older one that had been renovated. In a column he wrote for our diocesan paper soon before our oldest son's birth, Mitch describes the waiting that we—and the house—were doing:

Our house is very quiet this Saturday afternoon in winter. The small clock on the wall ticks with a loudness beyond its size. Kathy lies in our bedroom asleep, catching a much-needed nap. Only a few weeks are left now before the baby will be born. I have been stretched out here on the sofa reading, from a book, accounts of other people's birth experiences. It seems as if this aged house is growing an emptiness; it is silently waiting.

. . . This house, so long so old, will contain once again the adventures of a new life, will once again be brand new with a freshness like that on the first day of all. The scandal of it! That such an old, world-weary house should behave this way! The wisdom of it, too—that in a world where human hearts are so often hardened to such miracles (merely because they happen every day)—the wisdom of it that this old house should understand enough to know that sober joy is all that really matters, that waiting in final hope is right, is good.

Whether the news of the pregnancy is something a woman has been waiting to hear for months or years or is unexpected or at times even dreaded, her body and her world have already begun to change.

She may be already experiencing the physical stress of morning sickness—which some describe as the body's motion sickness because of the rapid changes and growth occurring within her—and her body will begin to feel different and change in shape before long, gradually becoming a mother's body. Like many other kinds of growth that she has faced and will, this experience involves a letting go of the familiar, of the way things are.

A "dying to self" is already beginning here, as classic spiritual writers would put it. In John's gospel when speaking about his upcoming death Jesus observes about all change and growth, ". . . unless a grain of wheat falls into the earth and dies, it remains just a single grain; but if it dies, it bears much fruit" (John 12:24).

In his book *Transitions: Making Sense of Life Changes,* William Bridges talks about endings as the first of three stages in any life transition, when *the way things have been* begins to shift. It is, he says, a time of disengagement, disidentification, disenchantment, and even disorientation. When *any* change begins in a person's life, there is a degree to which she doesn't know who she is any more; all she knows is who she's *not* any longer. The changes she is experiencing in pregnancy are the beginning for the new mother—whether this is her first pregnancy or not.

She is invited into nothing less than a journey of the spirit. A pregnancy is the most physically contemplative experience a human person can have. Especially once she feels the baby move within her, a mother's attention is regularly directed inward, no matter what is happening around her. It's as though her body is reminding her to look within—to look again, to *re-spect* herself—and see the beauty inside her and the miracle that she is capable of supporting and nourishing.

She is becoming an instrument of God's work of giving life and is being transformed from the inside out; her life will never be the same again. As she begins to appear more pregnant, the experience is both deeply internal *and* rather public, and she may be asked often about when the baby is due.

Many—if not most—pregnant women feel uncomfortable, awkward—perhaps even ugly at times. From sleeping to sitting down to getting dressed, almost every daily activity becomes trickier and more challenging for her. Late in the pregnancy she may wonder if she'll ever see her feet again! But there is far more than a physical experience at work here. While her body may feel more vulnerable in some ways—so that she needs to take more care in what she eats and drinks, for example—there is also an amazing wisdom at work within her body, knowing just what to do when needed.

This is a time filled with wonder, hope, and questions: Will the child be a boy or girl? While an increasing number of couples may know this in advance with the more routine use of ultrasound technology, there are still plenty of other questions to ponder: Will the baby be healthy? What or who will the baby look like? What should we name him or her? And even: will there be twins—or more?

In the meantime, the pregnant mother is sharing her body more completely with another person than even the intimate sharing involved in intercourse. This little person is completely dependent on her for physical survival and nourishment. What she takes into her body will nourish or—in the case of nicotine, alcohol, or other drugs—harm her baby. This realization in my first full-term pregnancy led me to a lasting interest in vitamins and good nutrition.

This union between mother and child is a powerful reminder of our closeness to God who is nearer than we know. Ellyn Sanna explains in her book, *Motherhood: A Spiritual Journey*:

> Birth-mothers . . . have all felt the fish-like movements within their pregnant bellies as their babies turn and twist, floating in the amniotic fluid. Having had that experience, these words of Catherine of Siena take on a richer and deeper meaning: "Then the soul is in God and God in the soul, just as the fish is in the sea and the sea in the fish." Marie of the Incarnation, a seventeenth-century woman who was both a mystic and a mother, also speaks of this encompassing union. Like the unborn baby who moves and curls serenely within the womb's cushion, we too are always sheltered by God's love. We have no "life or movement except by his life and his movement," says Marie. Mothers

who have experienced pregnancy know with their flesh the spiritual reality the saints describe. (p. 18)

INFERTILITY: WAITING IN HOPE

What about mothers—and couples—who have tried unsuccessfully to achieve a pregnancy? They have known a waiting that goes beyond any words. Society has come a long way from seeing "barrenness" as a curse from God, as it was referred to in the Old Testament. The medical community today knows far more than even a generation ago, but even today so much of the process of conception and fertility remains a mystery to scientists.

As more technology is available to help infertile couples, it is important that, as much as possible, the dignity, uniqueness, and holiness of the couple and their relationship are preserved. Many couples that have endured years of invasive medical treatment for infertility turn to adoption as the way to have their long-awaited child.

ADOPTION: THE GIFT OF LIFE

If a couple chooses to adopt, the waiting begins again. This is the realm of deep longing for a couple wanting a child and for a mother sharing a child with those who can offer a different future than what her child might otherwise face.

There are *at least* two mothers involved, and, perhaps, more. There's the "birth mother" and the "adoptive mother," both awkward terms but usually used for lack of better terminology. There may also be at least one foster mother who has been part of an adoptive child's life, as well as moms who still hold that child in their hearts after an unsuccessful adoption.

Today a woman considering giving up her child for adoption may have any number of important reasons for doing so—from being too young to problems with alcohol, drug, or physical abuse to poverty, depression, or other mental health issues. She also lives in a world where single mothers are far more common and have a higher profile and more social acceptance than in the past.

But if she does decide that adoption is the best choice for her child, she faces a lifetime of always holding her child in her heart, of mixed feelings every year on Mother's Day and every other day, of deciding what to say every time she is asked whether she has any children, as well as the possibility of The Call or The Letter sometime in the future if she doesn't keep in touch with the adoptive parents, a call or letter that asks, "Could you be my mother?"

In an open adoption—an increasingly common experience—she faces watching her child being raised by others who can give her child a different life than she could give, a wound for her that never fully heals. To say the least, she faces an extremely difficult choice, one that usually confronts her sooner than it hits either the birth father or the birth grandparents.

The adoptive mother's challenges are different but also considerable. If she's married, she and her husband may well have had problems with infertility, which may have entailed considerable medical treatment, and then they face the highly invasive process of a home study before qualifying for an adoption.

An adoptive mom who conducts home studies professionally commented that parents who have had other children biologically are amazed at how intrusive the process is, one that they never had to endure with their other children. Their whole lives are laid open to scrutiny, both before the adoption application can be approved and in the follow-up process, which can vary widely from agency to agency and state to state. But parents willingly undergo all this in order to get a child.

And then there is the waiting, waiting, waiting. One woman, longing to hear about a foreign adoption, described her phone line as the umbilical cord that connected her with her unborn infant in her psychologically pregnant state. The time often stretches on and on, usually for several years. Any child is certainly a gift, but adoptive parents report that they have a special sense of that reality.

One of the questions that loom for adoptive parents is how much to tell their children about their background. Several parents that I talked with said they had talked about their children being adopted from the very beginning, starting with children's books about adoption.

Another way to communicate about being adopted is to celebrate Gotcha Day, the day we "gotcha." A mother with two children from Korea explains how they've observed the day: "We recorded each of their arrivals on video, and my daughter saw that video last year on her Gotcha Day; it seemed to be very precious to her. When we celebrate Gotcha Day, we don't give any presents, like some families do, but we have a special dinner with parents and family and godparents. We either go to a Korean restaurant or have Korean food here at home."

Some families don't observe Gotcha Day, and some adoptive families don't talk much about the birth parents. How much a family knows and is willing to talk about the details about the adopted individual's family of birth *can* be difficult issues. Those issues may be that much harder in the case of an international adoption, where less may be known about the birth parents and where there is also the challenge of handling two different cultures as well as possible racial differences.

What does the experience of adoption have to say to *all* mothers and their spirituality? More than it may seem at first.

While adoption is rare in the Jewish scriptures, St. Paul's letters remind his readers that we are *all* adopted children of God, especially in his letter to the Romans: "For those who are led by the Spirit of God are children of God. For you did not receive a spirit of slavery to fall back into fear, but you received a spirit of adoption, through which we cry, 'Abba, Father!'" (8:14–15).

In a very real sense, we are *all* adopted in the family of faith. We are warmly welcomed into God's arms and God's family and given full rights as heirs, not just second-class status—even though that acceptance is a gift and a grace, not something we deserve. To imagine that we are each waited for and longed for at great expense by God and then welcomed as an adopted child is a powerful image indeed.

BAPTISM: SACRAMENT OF BELONGING

Whether as an infant or as an adult, whether waiting and preparing for it for weeks or months or longer, Baptism is where every Christian life begins. Through the pouring of water or immersion in it, the one being baptized is joined to Christ and to the whole Christian community.

The water of Baptism is the same water that makes up the majority of our bodies and of all living creatures, the same water that surrounds us *in utero*, and the same water without which life would not be possible on this planet. It's also the same water with which mothers daily wash dishes and counters, hands and faces, as well as bathe their children, or take a shower or bath. And it's a cool, refreshing drink on a dry, hot day.

Water can also be destructive: if the tub overflows or the pipes break or the river floods its banks or if someone drowns, it can be a source of damage and death as well as life. And, as we'll explore further in the season of Holy Week and Easter, we know that any kind of washing is a process of dying and rising, first making a bigger mess before whatever is being cleaned—whether it's hair or floor— is clean and renewed.

Water is, therefore, a sign of both dying and of life for the Christian community, of each Christian being called to die and rise with Christ, to "put on Christ," as St. Paul puts it. Sometimes we also call it "christening," because it's about the process of *becoming* Christ.

The one being baptized is being welcomed into a *community* of believers, just as the new child is welcomed into the community of the immediate and extended family and into the culture as a whole. That person will not be a Christian in isolation, just as none of us are in isolation in the rest of our lives. The web of relationships around us helps all of us in the messy, continuing process of dying and rising with Christ and of helping share the light of faith that we have been given, a light which in turn came from others who have shared this faith with us.

Whether blessing ourselves with holy water when coming into church—in the name of the Trinity in which we were baptized—or simply washing our hands, water renews us and reminds us that we are not alone as we live out our Baptism by becoming Christ's love in our daily lives.

MOTHERS SPEAK

Listen as mothers talk about the themes of Advent in their experience:

I found out about my first pregnancy on the Feast of the Annunciation. My reaction was, "How is this possible?" for I had been told that I wouldn't be able to conceive or bear children. When I first started feeling the baby move within, I remember one of the readings was from the psalm, "I knew you before I knit you together in your mother's womb." My pregnancy brought scripture alive in a way I hadn't heard it before.

After the birth as I looked at my son, I marveled at the idea of being created in the image and likeness of God. And then the overwhelming awareness that we had been given this little soul to raise set in.

In my pregnancies I felt responsible, creative, blessed, watched, celebrated, unsure, graced, amazed, tired, and filled with life. I loved being pregnant, loved the conversations with colleagues, family, and strangers. It was a time I really felt intimately involved with creation and the act of creating. I secretly felt sadness for my husband because he would never know this kind of intimacy. I was so happy to be a woman!

The most powerful experience I have had as a mother was being a foster mother for several years and being involved not only in nurturing but also in the legal aspects of protecting "my children." I was forced to *choose* between two little ones that I had for a year and a half. They were like sister and brother, so not only was my heart torn into agonizing shreds, these kids also lost one another—another loss for them. The boy became my adopted son, and the girl I still hear from.

I wish I had been told that it's okay not to be the perfect mother. As an adoptive mom I've always felt some instinct or some "level of love" that would automatically have made me a better mom. I'll never know, as I was not blessed with the pregnancy/birth experience; but I do know that however your children are given to you by God, all you can do is your best and that screw-ups along the way are part and parcel of motherhood.

MODELS FROM THE TRADITION

When we look to the Christian tradition, to the saints and others for models of both waiting and the communal aspect of mothers' spirituality, three examples that emerge are Ruth and Naomi, the Desert Mothers, and St. Monica.

Ruth and Naomi, in the book of Ruth in the Old Testament, show us a strong friendship and a support between women rarely seen in all of literature, especially between mother- and daughter-in-law. Both are widowed as the book begins; Naomi's husband had moved with her to Moab at a time of famine, where she had given birth to two sons, and Ruth, a Moabite woman, had married one of those sons. Orpah, the other daughter-law, whose husband also has died, wisely decides that she will stay in her native land and culture.

Ruth, however, decides to join her mother-in-law in her journey back to her Jewish relatives and community, and now Ruth faces the prospect of being an outcast in a foreign land. She tells Naomi, "Do not press me to leave you or to turn back from following you! Where you go, I will go; Where you lodge, I will lodge; your people shall be my people, and your God my God" (Ruth 1:16).

As women alone, without husband or son to take care of them, both Ruth and Naomi are at risk in their culture in many ways—socially, economically, and physically. Their journey together into the unknown and, finally, to a new marriage for Ruth and new life for both of them is a warm portrait of the support that women and mothers can be for one another in so many ways. We need one another as women, not because we are weak but because we are strong.

It was the strength of their shared faith in Christ which led the **Desert Mothers**, who were not mothers in the usual sense of the word, to help bring to birth a deep and fresh look at living the gospel of Jesus.

Along with the better-known Desert Fathers, or *abbas*, the Desert Mothers, or *ammas*, were a group of individuals who, as Christianity gained social acceptance in the fourth century, stepped away from the mainstream of society to more radically live the life of simplicity, self-denial, prayer, and generosity to the poor called for in the gospels.

These individuals usually lived in communities, in the deserts of Egypt, Syria, Persia, and present-day Turkey, but also throughout the Mediterranean world and the British isles, mainly from the third to the sixth centuries. What little we have left of the writing and thinking of these *ammas* shows a clarity of insight about spiritual topics that is being rediscovered today.

Laura Swan, OSB, author of *The Forgotten Desert Mothers*, comments on her own experience of studying these women and how they helped her confront a difficult time in her own life:

When I encountered the ammas, they made sense of the desert in my life. . . . The desert requires us to explore our crisis of personal meaning. The ammas show us how the work of our desert moves us through integration toward authenticity. The fruit of the desert struggle is abundant life and deep abiding joy. (p. 167)

The Desert Mothers remind us that we all can possess the qualities of simplicity of vision, of seeing what is really important in our lives, and the strength that sees mothers through the difficult times—our own deserts, that may *seem* barren and unfruitful—as part of our gifts as mothers.

Just as prayer was an important part of the life of the Desert Mothers, it was also central for **St. Monica** (332–387), the mother of St. Augustine of Hippo, whom we know only through her son's famous book, *The Confessions.* In it he describes her persistence in praying and hoping for her son's eventual conversion to Christianity. She seems to have worried over her son's behavior and his spiritual welfare to a degree to rival many of the most persistent or "pushy" moms we may know. Robert Ellsberg describes her this way in his book *All Saints: Daily Reflections on Saints, Prophets, and Witnesses for Our Time:*

> She did not cease to suffer on his behalf, praying constantly for his conversion and weeping over his sins. Finally, a sympathetic bishop reassured her: "Go now, I beg of you: it is not possible that the son of so many tears should perish." (p. 369)

Monica is a model for us of waiting and of faithful prayer as a mother, which is at times all we have left as a way to reach our children when they have left the shelter of our homes and our arms.

SCRIPTURE FOR REFLECTION

*As we reflect on our own lives as mothers and the role of waiting and shar-
ing with other women, the following passages may be helpful. Please try to
take some time with one or more of these passages and with the questions
following them. You may prefer to reflect on these with other mothers.*

In the sixth month the angel Gabriel was sent by God to a
town in Galilee called Nazareth, to a virgin engaged to a man
whose name was Joseph, of the house of David. The virgin's
name was Mary. And he came to her and said, "Greetings,
favored one! The Lord is with you." But she was much per-
plexed by his words and pondered what sort of greeting this
might be. The angel said to her, "Do not be afraid, Mary, for
you have found favor with God. And now, you will conceive
in your womb and bear a son, and you will name him Jesus.
He will be great, and will be called the Son of the Most
High, and the Lord God will give to him the throne of his
ancestor David. He will reign over the house of Jacob forever, and of his kingdom there will be no end." Mary said to
the angel, "How can this be, since I am a virgin?" The angel
said to her, "The Holy Spirit will come upon you, and the
power of the Most High will overshadow you; therefore the
child to be born will be holy; he will be called Son of God.
And now, your relative Elizabeth in her old age has also con-
ceived a son; and this is the sixth month for her who was said
to be barren. For nothing will be impossible with God."
Then Mary said, "Here am I, the servant of the Lord; let it
be with me according to your word." Then the angel de-
parted from her. (Luke 1:26–38)

—*How have you reacted to unexpected news or to being called on to do
something you weren't expecting?*

—*To what have you said "yes" to God's Spirit in your life? And to what have you said "no"?*

—*Is there anything in your life right now that God asks you to trust in without fully understanding it?*

When Elizabeth heard Mary's greeting, the child leaped in her womb. And Elizabeth was filled with the Holy Spirit and exclaimed with a loud cry, "Blessed are you among women, and blessed is the fruit of your womb. And why has this happened to me, that the mother of my Lord comes to me? For as soon as I heard the sound of your greeting, the child in my womb leaped for joy. And blessed is she who believed that there would be a fulfillment of what was spoken to her by the Lord." And Mary said, "My soul magnifies the Lord, and my spirit rejoices in God my Savior, for he has looked with favor on the lowliness of his servant. Surely, from now on all generations will call me blessed; for the Mighty One has done great things for me, and holy is his name. His mercy is for those who fear him from generation to generation. He has shown strength with his arm; he has scattered the proud in the thoughts of their hearts. He has brought down the powerful from their thrones, and lifted up the lowly; he has filled the hungry with good things, and sent the rich away empty. He has helped his servant Israel, in remembrance of his mercy, according to the promise he made to our ancestors, to Abraham and to his descendants forever."

And Mary remained with her about three months and then returned to her home. (Luke 1:41–56)

—*To whom would you turn with big news in your life? How does that person help you see how much God is at work in you?*

—*How do you see God at work in your life now? How is that experience connected with the way God has acted in others' lives and in scripture?*

O LORD, you have searched me and known me. You know when I sit down and when I rise up; you discern my thoughts from far away. You search out my path and my lying down, and are acquainted with all my ways. Even before a word is on my tongue, O LORD, you know it completely. You hem me in, behind and before, and lay your hand upon me. Such knowledge is too wonderful for me; it is so high that I cannot attain it. . . . For it was you who formed my inward parts; you knit me together in my mother's womb. I praise you, for I am fearfully and wonderfully made. Wonderful are your works; that I know very well. My frame was not hidden from you, when I was being made in secret, intricately woven in the depths of the earth. (Psalms 139:1–6, 13–15)

—*Picture yourself being "knit" in your mother's womb and imagine God's delight in you—then and now.*
—*Who has been the best reflection of God's tender love for you in your life?*
—*Try to imagine how much better God knows you than your best friend does. What is your reaction to that awareness?*

Other Scripture Passages to Explore
1 Samuel 2:1–10—The song of Hannah, mother of Samuel, which Mary's Magnificat will later echo.

Psalm 63:1–9—A song of waiting and longing for God's presence and help.

Questions for Individual or Group Reflection
What are you waiting for in your life right now?

Where do you experience darkness and where do you experience light?

How have the experiences of infertility, pregnancy, or adoption brought you closer to God?

Who is a support for you right now? How can you strengthen or build that support, if you need to?

Resources for This Season
The following are some resources related to the themes explored here; full information on these can be found at the end of this book.

Elizabeth Ministry
MOMS
Bridges, *Transitions*
Chittister, *The Story of Ruth*
Houselander, *A Child in Winter*
Nelson, *To Dance with God*
Swan, *The Forgotten Desert Mothers*

Chapter Two

CHRISTMAS AND EPIPHANY
A Child Is Born to Us

M ARCY WAS STILL TRYING TO BELIEVE IT. SHE AND CARL
actually had a son! The past few months of the pregnancy now
seemed like a blur: the prepared childbirth classes and the
shower that her friends from work had given her, even her
memories of the time in the hospital were now beginning to
fade. She couldn't recall when she had been this much in awe—
of anything or anyone. Little Ian had an amazing smile and incredible fingers and toes—so tiny and intricate and beautiful.

She had so many feelings that she didn't know where to begin to reflect on this experience: there was certainly excitement
and joy, as well as a bit of panic about not knowing what to do
next. She also worried about doing anything less than her very
best for this child whose life was now in her and her husband's
hands. She kept praying, "Loving God, give us all the graces and
gifts we need to help Ian be the best person he can be."

WHAT IS THIS SEASON?

A newborn child *is* a wonder, one to which we are naturally
drawn. At the center of the season of Christmas and

Epiphany is the newborn Jesus, born both in Bethlehem so many years ago and born anew in our hearts and in our lives.

Beyond the lights and the decorations, the countdown of shopping days and all the TV specials waits the quiet, awe-inspiring feast of Emmanuel, God-with-us, a newborn in a manger who is the Son of God. In a cattle trough, amid the smelly animals and the hay—because there was no room in the busy world around him—lies the long-awaited Savior. Hopefully, at this hectic time of year we can keep the commercial interests at arm's length long enough to focus our attention on the simple yet profound scene that lies before us.

Like the shepherds, we come to adore this child who has come as *the* Christmas present, the Incarnation (God made flesh) or, as one child put it, God's show-and-tell. The early Christians celebrated this reality at Christmas when others around them were celebrating the birthday of the unconquered Sun on December 25, the date of the winter solstice on the Julian calendar, then in use.

It is likely that the feast of the Epiphany, or manifestation, of Christ actually predates Christmas as a celebration, and in the Eastern rites of Christianity this day commemorates Jesus' Baptism as well as his birth, while in the West it focuses on the visit of the magi who bring gifts for the newborn King. Epiphany shows us that the light of Christ is not just a glow from a stable for a few; the star leading those from the East reminds us that Jesus is for *all* people and *all* times, even for us Gentiles (non-Jews) and outsiders.

Indeed, as we take a closer look, not only are the magi outsiders but so are the shepherds; they were among the lowest of the social classes of the time. Even Mary and Joseph end up on the fringes of the crowd that has come to Bethlehem to be recorded for the census. Like any good mother, the season of Christmas and Epiphany reminds us to look out for the outsiders, the little ones, those otherwise neglected, and to make sure that they are not forgotten.

As we come as mothers to behold the newborn Jesus, we know that a birth *is* exciting and wonderful, and that it's also more complex than that. A new child is challenging and tiring for a mom, and a birth brings questions and fears to her mind: Will this child be healthy and safe? Will I be able to give this child all that he or she needs? What will this child become? With Mary, we can only wonder.

FROM THE TRADITION

What practices from the Christian tradition can help enhance our appreciation of the season of Christmas and Epiphany and of the Incarnation in our lives?

The **Nativity scene** or **creche** is a powerful reminder to us of God made flesh in Jesus. Its origins go back to Francis of Assisi, the simple and poor saint, who in 1223 wanted to help the farmers of the town of Greccio to imagine the first Christmas. He had them build a stable, and there, amidst real animals, they celebrated the feast of Christmas that year.

In many homes the nativity scene is a key focus during the days of Advent, but the infant may be absent until Christmas Eve, when a child will bring it to the manger, perhaps as a Christmas carol is sung. Some families also like to let children in the family add straw or small strips of paper to the manger each night during Advent if the children have been kind to others that day, so that they help make a softer "bed" for the infant Jesus when he is placed there. Other families place the wise men around the room and have them "travel" a bit every day until they "arrive" on the feast of the Epiphany.

Nativity scenes come in all shapes and sizes, with a wide variety of "characters"; some people even collect creches from various places. But whether simple or elegant, a manger scene is an excellent way to help the child in all of us imagine Love Made Flesh. The creche also helps mothers remember the incomparable wonder of the experience of *each* birth and the true miracle that any child is.

This value of the **respect for all of life** was articulated well by the late Cardinal Joseph Bernardin of Chicago, in a series of talks in 1983, as he helped call attention to a consistent ethic of life, sometimes called a "seamless garment." He argued that, while issues from abortion to capital punishment to euthanasia to warfare and social justice all pose unique challenges to us today, they are also linked because the Christian responsibility is to uphold the dignity of human life wherever it is challenged. Mothers have known this truth in their bones and have acted on it through endless generations.

As we celebrate new life, it is good for us to remember that the **Twelve Days of Christmas** are not just a Christmas carol; they begin on Christmas Day and stretch until the traditional date for the Epiphany, January 6. (This feast is now celebrated on the Sunday between January 2 and January 8.) This time reminds us that the Christmas season isn't over on Christmas Day, as the retailers would have us believe; it's just beginning. And it's a time to continue to celebrate being together with family and friends—in simple and inexpensive ways. Our culture has largely lost the ability to just enjoy each other; however, mothers know that little is needed other than the people they love and maybe some time and food to share with one another.

One way to celebrate during these days is to have a **house blessing**, which is traditional for the feast of Epiphany, perhaps because just as the Christ was made manifest to the world, so the home—as the domestic church—is a place where God is made manifest to the world. This can be as simple as a time to give thanks for our family's home and to offer a prayer for those without a place to live, or it can involve going from room to room, blessing each in turn and praying for all that happens there. One tradition is to mark a doorway in chalk with crosses, the year, and the initials of the traditional names for the three magi: Caspar, Melchior, and Balthasar. (So, for example, for the year 2010, the markings would be "20+C+M+B+10.")

Our homes are indeed far more holy than we usually realize, and the way that the space is laid out within our homes can make a big difference in the ways we gather, for meals and other occasions, and how we interact with each other. Often it's only when we are moving or later return to a house where we used to live that we begin to see just how that house helped shape our lives and to realize that it *is* a holy place because of what has happened within it, simply and humbly, day in and day out.

Within the twelve days of Christmas are a couple of feast days that can seem at first not to fit at all in this season: they are feasts of **martyrs**, those who were killed for their faith (from the Greek for "witness"). The remembrance of St. Stephen, the first martyr, is the day after Christmas, and the commemoration of the Holy Innocents is on December 28. In the book of Acts we read that Stephen was a deacon, involved in helping with the practical needs of the early Christian community, and that he was stoned to death for his faith by those who were persecuting the Christians.

The story of the innocents—who are not exactly martyrs because they died unknowingly in the place of Jesus—is directly related to the Epiphany. The wise men, having been warned in a dream after seeing Jesus, did not go back to tell King Herod what they had found in Bethlehem. Matthew's gospel tells us:

> When Herod realized that he had been deceived by the magi, he became furious. He ordered the massacre of all the boys in Bethlehem and its vicinity two years old and under, in accordance with the time he had ascertained from the magi. Then was fulfilled what had been said through Jeremiah the prophet: "A voice was heard in Ramah, sobbing and loud lamentation; Rachel weeping for her children, and she would not be consoled, since they were no more." (Matthew 2:16–18)

What do these deaths have to do with the season of Christmas? For one, they are a reminder of the violent world into which Jesus—and we—were born and a world in which death may result from living the truth of one's faith or even from being in the wrong place at the wrong time. And because mothers' spirituality is communal, as we have already seen, the fact that today there are still far too many children dying senselessly from war and poverty in our world is a concern for *all* mothers.

The martyrs in the early Church were seen by the community as part of the birth of the Christian faith; the saying was, "The blood of martyrs is the seed of the church." The anniversaries of their deaths were considered to be their birthdays into heaven and were remembered and honored. While mothers don't usually die for their faith or their children, there *is* a kind of dying that is a part of motherhood that we will explore later when we look at Holy Week.

Another aspect of the Catholic tradition connected to martyrs and saints is that of **relics**, a topic that has often been misunderstood. A relic is either a part of the body of a saint or martyr or something that has been touched or used by that person.

Although the notion of a relic may seem quite distant from mothers in the contemporary world, a second look reveals more connections to their experience. Consider a lock of hair in a baby book, a bronzed baby shoe, or even a valuable autograph or guitar from a rock star; as individuals and as a culture we like to "hold onto" objects that remind us of important people and the past. Unfortunately, in the medieval culture relics too often took on a sense of magic, but when relics are used properly they continue to be a way for us to "stay in touch" with those in the past who were important in the *tradition*, the "handing on" of faith. Mothers are often the ones to treasure the objects that help hold the history of their family, and they understand the importance of touch in all kinds of ways, as we will see next.

MOTHERS' SPIRITUALITY IS *INCARNATIONAL*

As Mary cared for the newborn Jesus, did she know that the most spiritual action she could take toward her God was also the most practical and physical one, that of holding and caring for the infant in her arms? We'll never know. What women *do* know is that as human persons we are whole, all-of-a-piece, not just a dualistic tension between body and soul, spirit and flesh, as our culture has too often assumed.

Is there a mother who hasn't been involved with not only fixing meals but also with wiping bottoms or noses, kissing owies, and even cleaning up after a baby that has spit up or after someone who has been sick? We can't seem to get away from others' bodies, as well as our own. As we deal with bodies—with the way the real world is—we also encounter the realm of the spirit and mind, and we *know* they are not two separate realms but, rather, intrinsically linked.

The rather recent holistic awareness among some thinkers—that physical exercise helps reduce emotional stress, for example, which in turn impacts our spirituality—wouldn't be news to our grandmothers and the women who came before them; they knew these connections within the human person intuitively. They saw that the realities that we call spiritual—faith, love, forgiveness, and grace—come to us through our bodies or not at all. In fact, as we will see later, mothers have tended to use images and stories in talking about their spiritually to help them make sense of what can otherwise seem fairly abstract and theoretical.

A mother may begin to experience clues about seeing herself and others holistically—not just as a person possessing a body and a spirit, but as *one seamless, whole being* whose mind, body, and spirit are so clearly interconnected—during pregnancy. For example, her psychological and emotional experiences of stress can affect her baby in various ways, including physically, so that a mom has an extra reason to take care of herself well during these days.

Mothers tend to use all their senses in their tender care and love for others and God. Whether it's their sense of *smell* ("Something's burning!") or of *hearing* ("What are you doing in there?") or *tasting* the infant's food before feeding him or her so that the food is just the right temperature, the spiritual reality of love happens for mothers *through their bodies*. Not only do moms use their *sight* to watch for problems for their little ones, they're also rewarded with scenes such as a child of whatever age peacefully asleep at the end of the day or a little one cuddling a doll or a pet just as that child has in turn been held.

Touch is perhaps the most important sense of all for mothers. From the early bonding with a newborn to a gentle grasp of a dying person's hand, mothers know that the sense of touch is the most powerful way for us to reach one another and to communicate our love without a word. And then there's also mothers' famous sixth sense, the intuitive knowing that goes beyond the physical evidence to just *know* sometimes, even in the dark and the silence.

Mary Gordon, in her novel *Men and Angels,* talks about how bodily *and* holy a mother's love is, as only a novelist can:

> She looked at the clock. It was two-thirty; soon the children would be home. She waited for the sound of their arrival as if she were dressed for a party, listening for a taxi. No one had told her what it would be like, the way she loved her children. What a thing of the body it was, as physically rooted as sexual desire, but without its edge of danger. The urge to touch one's child, she often thought, was like, and wasn't like, the hunger that one felt to touch a lover. . . . Once the children were in the house, the air became more vivid and more heated: every object in the house grew more alive. How I love you, she always wanted to say, and you can never know it. I would die for you without a thought. You have given to my life its sheerest, its profoundest pleasure. But she could never say that. Instead, she would say, "How was school?" "Was lunch all right?" "Did you have your math test?" (p. 16)

Although our love as mothers involves our bodies as well as our hearts, we also know that the culture in which we live and the advertising that surrounds us tend to split the human person and to entice us to see ourselves in a disconnected way. This tendency has severe consequences, both for us as individuals as well as for our society as a whole.

Our sexuality, for example, is less than healthy as long as we think that it involves *parts* of ourselves rather than *our whole beings*; sex is more closely linked to our spirituality than we've even begun to acknowledge. We have a key role as mothers in helping our children appreciate their sexuality as an important part of their whole selves, not as something to be ashamed of. And we can also help them understand the difference between good touch and secret or bad touch— that their bodies and their whole selves are to be respected and not violated by anyone.

Mothers also can have a strong sense of how poorly our culture has treated Mother Earth, which is in turn closely related to how we treat each other. As we begin to recover a sense of balance and appreciation of the cycle of life, we can begin to listen and see what we have been doing to our planet. But when we treat it with a lack of respect or without an awareness of how all of life is interrelated, then we fail to have the necessary respect for those peoples or creatures who may be different from us.

Mothers know about love, and they know that they don't love bodies *or* spirits; they love *whole persons*.

ACHIEVING A BALANCE

How can this incarnational, holistic quality of mothers' spirituality, that is so needed and so valuable in our world, get out of balance at times and be less than healthy?

On the one hand, as mothers we can tend to get *too caught up in the material*, in the details, and miss the forest for the trees. We cover the details in life fairly well—we have to or often they don't get handled. But that can mean that we can forget to see the miracles that are all around us.

Mothers can get so taken up in the desire to look attractive and to make our homes pleasant that we forget to take the time to appreciate that what happens *inside* us and *within* our homes is the most important and "attractive." Some mothers may need to spend less time worrying about their makeup or losing a few pounds or shopping to redecorate a room and, instead, take a bit more time for wonder and prayer, for centering and focusing themselves—even and especially when that seems an impossible luxury. Paradoxically, our desire for beauty can distract us from true Beauty if we don't center ourselves well enough.

On the other hand, as mothers we can forget to *treat ourselves to the goodness of the created world around us.* For example, we might not buy that bouquet of flowers at the store because it doesn't seem practical or "sensible," when in fact it may be exactly the opposite. God created the goodness of the created world for our delight and enjoyment; mothers can spend so much time working—because there's so much to be done, it seems—that we can forget to enjoy what God has given us for our delight.

The more that mothers can understand, claim, and articulate—for themselves and others—their experience of the interconnectedness of the material and the spiritual aspects of our life and of all that our culture has tended to separate, the more we can help to heal our fractured world for all of us.

LABOR AND DELIVERY: A NEW LIFE

In this season of new life, one of the key experiences of mothers that suggests itself for our consideration is that of labor and birth. For all that scientists now know about human development and much of what happens in childbirth, we are still not able to predict when labor will begin. A mother's body shows its own unique rhythm and pacing as it prepares for the important work of giving birth.

Here we encounter a clear example of the tension between separating and integrating the human person. While for many centuries births happened largely at home with midwives usually in attendance, in the last couple centuries or so the process of birth came under the scientific care of doctors in hospitals. And while many women and children who might have died in childbirth in the past are now able to survive, something was also lost in the process of moving childbirth to a modern medical setting.

What had been a natural process, a powerful spiritual and relational reality with a physical component, now was seen as a primarily physical, medical problem to be solved, with the baby as a "product" that needed to be delivered safely. Many women giving birth in a hospital setting have reported feeling alienated from their bodies, and many have stories of how the medical situation took priority over their emotional or other needs in giving birth.

Today, hospitals and the medical community are more responsive to couples and families and to their well-being. There is a move to more completely acknowledge and work with the relational dynamics involved in a birth. Good psychology and spirituality are increasingly being seen as good medical practice as well.

Every aspect of labor and delivery is complex and gives us reason to wonder at a God that creates us and helps bring us to birth in an amazing way. For example, anthropologist Ashley Montagu, in his fascinating book *Touching: The Human Significance of the Skin*, explains that the hours of contractions in human labor help to stimulate the various systems of the soon-to-be newborn, much like the licking that every other mammal mother gives newborns so that they are better able to survive outside the womb.

He comments on another difference in the human newborn:

> . . . the passage through the 4 inches of the birth canal is the most hazardous journey a human being ever takes. The evidence suggests that the human fetus is born before its gestation is completed. The rate of growth of the brain is proceeding at such a pace during the last month of pregnancy that its continuation within the womb would render birth impossible. Hence, the survival of the fetus and the mother requires the termination of gestation within the womb when the limit of head size compatible with birth has been attained, and long before maturation occurs. (p. 43)

Montagu goes on to say that the level of independence that most other mammals have at birth is only reached by the human infant at about nine months of age, when the baby has spent as much time outside the uterus as it did inside. If it *is* true that we are all born "half-baked," in a sense, that would especially help to explain the importance of what we now know about bonding after birth.

Bonding is a dance that a mother and a newborn do—with their eyes, with their bodies in touching and holding, and, ultimately, with their emotions. Specialists in bonding tell us that mother—and father—and child are actually helping to finish building the baby's brain through the second year.

During a child's first eight months, the number of neural connections more than doubles; after that their production slows considerably. But the brain's right hemisphere—which handles emotions and empathy—is being strongly influenced. Babies are especially sensitive during the first couple years to how their caregivers respond emotionally, from engaging expressions to a soothing voice.

This crucial process of bonding gets interrupted in a highly complex way with a situation of adoption or foster care. Without a responsive and consistent reaction from the caregiver, what may result is avoidant or ambivalent attachment, where the infant is protecting him- or herself from the pain of rejection that she or he may have experienced in the past. We are still learning a great deal about how this process of bonding works and what can be done to repair inadequate bonding, but we do know that the early caregivers, especially the mother, have an amazing impact on this new little person.

But first comes the birth itself. "When a woman is in labor, she has pain, because her hour has come," John's gospel reminds us. "But when her child is born, she no longer remembers the anguish because of the joy of having brought a human being into the world" (John 16:21). Ask any mother to tell you about her first birth (or any other), and you will get quite a story, perhaps with some memories of pain, but with far more joy as she recalls it now.

The births of each of our sons are precious memories for me, especially the night our oldest son was born, since he was the first. I remember thinking, after a fairly hard labor, that God must look at each of us with even more wonder and delight *every moment of every day* than what we experience in first beholding our firstborn child—a depth of love that it's hard to even begin to imagine.

There is a long Catholic tradition of the churching of women, a blessing of women after childbirth. It has its roots in the purification after childbirth mentioned in the Old Testament, but there are no references whatsoever now to childbirth being unclean. In the Book of Blessings this special ritual consists of a scripture reading, a psalm, a prayer of thanksgiving, and the following blessing:

O God, author and sustainer of human life, from your goodness your servant [name] has received the joy of becoming a mother. Graciously accept thanks and give ear to our prayers: defend this mother and child from every evil, be their companion along their pathway through life, and welcome them one day into the joys of your eternal home. (McBrien, p. 317)

STEPMOTHERS AND FOSTER MOTHERS: A COMPLEX LOVE

The Christian tradition of seeing Joseph, Mary's husband, as the foster father of Jesus—since Jesus was the Son of God—raises the topic of those parents whose link to a child isn't biological.

Stepmothers—now more likely the result of a past divorce rather than the death of the biological mom—come with an automatic "bad rap" in every folk literature of every country in the world, and they may find that they have to live down a reputation they didn't have anything to do with building. If a stepmother's presence *is* due to divorce, she can symbolize the death of any dream the children may have had of their parents finally reuniting; if the children's mother has died, she still contends with what some have called "Ghosts at the Table."

The experience of step parenting is increasingly common today, and it is probably the most complicated family role of all—even tougher than that of a single parent. The first two years of this experience are almost always ones of turmoil and conflict—even in healthy families, researchers tell us—and the adjustment for everyone involved typically takes from eighteen months to four years.

One of the biggest questions facing a woman in this setting is her role with the children. A foster mother or step-mom *isn't* the mother—the children already have one—and she's more than a friend. Many successful mothers in these roles have decided that they will be advisors and trusted adults to children who can use the extra support.

In *Keys to Successful Step-Mothering*, Philippa Greene Mulford suggests that timing can be everything in this role:

> Sometimes being a stepmother means stepping *into* a child's life to advise, guide, or take control of a situation biological parents are unable or unwilling to deal with. At other time, being a stepmother means stepping *aside* to allow children time alone with their father, for instance. Then there are times when a stepmother is wise to step *out*, such as when disagreements arise over discipline or other matters that create a serious impasse between the stepmother and stepchild or the stepmother and her husband. Knowing which direction to step at any given moment can be difficult, indeed. (p. 16)

Both stepmothers and foster mothers—as well as the adoptive moms we have already considered—remind us that there is far more to motherhood than just giving birth. So much of *any* mother's life is deciding "which direction to step" in love for her children's and her own sake. Part of what helps her make these decisions well is a strong sense of prayer and an ability to listen for God's voice as it reveals itself in her life.

GRANDMOTHERS: AN EXTRA GENERATION OF LOVE

Although Simeon and Anna weren't really grandparents to Jesus, the feast of the Presentation of Jesus in the Temple, celebrated on February 2, just after the season of Christmas

and Epiphany, reminds us of the role that an older generation plays in the lives of children and their mothers. When
they see and hold the child Jesus, both Simeon and Anna are
clearly grateful for the gift of this child and know what a
privilege that is—for them and for all generations. (See
"Scripture for Reflection" below.)

To step into the role of grandmother is to relinquish
some of the job description of mother—even more than it
has already been modified with grown children. Now the next
generation can take on the responsibility of being mom and
dad, and grandma is called to step back and to be a support.

As some of my friends have begun to be grandmothers,
they also report an unparalleled level of gratitude for, and
delight in, these little ones. It's not just being able to hand
them back to their parents when they become too much, as
we often hear; they find that their grandchildren offer them
a second chance at a wonderful nurturing role with less day-
to-day pressure and hopefully a bit more wisdom and experience. There is far more freedom, they tell me, to just enjoy
the grandchildren *as they are.*

That role, however, becomes far more complex for an
increasing number of heroic grandparents who find themselves raising their grandchildren into their retirement years
because their children are unable to do so. These grandparents are a deep source of grace for these children, who may
not realize that blessing until many years later.

Grandparents of any kind—even the honorary ones
found in a neighbor or friend, since grandparents may be a
voice on the telephone for some mobile young families—are
a resource that mothers know they need: those valuable other
people in their children's lives who can cherish them, perhaps
even serve as mentors, and remind all of us of the wondrous
grace of the younger generation. Some ethnic groups, such

as the African American community, have been especially rich in a sense of what some have called "othermothers," and there is much there from which we can all learn.

CONFIRMATION: SACRAMENT OF COMMITMENT

Just as the infant Jesus was brought to the temple, Christian parents through the centuries have brought their children for Baptism and Confirmation. Christian initiation has varied somewhat throughout Christian history, but the sacrament of Confirmation was originally linked to the sacrament of Baptism and is gradually being reconnected to the sacraments of initiation such as Eucharist throughout our country. Confirmation has always been connected to Baptism for Christians in the Eastern rites and also for those in the West who become Catholics when adults through the Rite of Christian Initiation of Adults (RCIA).

The blessing with chrism (oils that have been blessed) was done by the bishop during the Baptismal rite in the ancient Church in the countries of present-day Europe. But when the bishop was unable to be at every Baptism, what gradually became the sacrament of Confirmation waited for his visit. It was linked to the outpouring of the gifts of the Holy Spirit, strengthening the one being confirmed to live out the Christian faith—so that the life of faith would be much more than just going through the motions. This was celebrated with the support of a sponsor, who might be one of the godparents from Baptism.

Sponsors and godparents are examples of those other people mothers know they need in their children's lives, people who will help support, inspire, and guide their children, just as Mary experienced the support of several important people soon after Jesus' birth. We can help choose some of these people in our children's lives, but some will just happen through God's grace.

These people can help foster the seven gifts of the Holy Spirit in our children: wisdom, understanding, counsel, fortitude, knowledge, piety, and fear (or awe) of the Lord. We will consider these qualities, especially wisdom, and the Holy Spirit further when we explore the season of Pentecost, but these gifts are ways to help us to appreciate God's presence in our lives and in our world and to respond to that presence more fully and generously. As our children grow and develop, we begin to see more and more that these children belong first and foremost to God and that they are only on loan to us. Our role, then, is one of helping to guide them and of praying for other healthy guides and teachers in their lives.

Like the water used in Baptism, the key sign used in this and the sacraments of the Anointing of the Sick and Holy Orders is that of anointing, covering part of the body with oil. Oil was used in ancient times both to heal and refresh and to mark as special and holy. Mothers often use oil or lotion on babies and children as well as on themselves, to help with dry skin or to protect from too much sun. Not only does oil renew our skin and make it feel softer, but it also smells good, reminding us how pleasing we are to God, who made us just the way we are.

Aunt Jo

MOTHERS SPEAK

Again we hear from mothers and their experience as it relates to the themes of this Christmas/Epiphany season:

The most powerful experience as a mother for me was giving birth and the experience of bodily health during pregnancy, the feeling of abundance and closeness to the fertility of earth and the rhythms of life. This was the most creative experience of my life.

God speaks to me and teaches me through my children—not the God of high and lofty thoughts, but an earthy God whose feet are planted in the soil of our lives. Being a mom permeates all of my life; it's not something I can easily isolate. Being a mother is part of an ongoing conversation between being a wife, a minister, a friend, etc. They interact, they conflict, they coexist, they are like hands working the clay of my life. They do not exist in neat, separate boxes, but are found in the messy but active life that gives shape to the clay in the potter's studio. Sometimes the pot is great; at other times I just have to give up and start again. For me, this is the experience of living the Paschal mystery, the dying and rising of Christ in my life.

I continue to be filled with awe and wonder at the beauty of people, of the incredible ways my heart grows larger from each person that has entered my life and whom I have been gifted with loving. I think it is because of little ones that I have learned to stay gentle . . . and know of God's care-full touch. Holding an infant, a young child, has taught me how incredible and limitless is God's love . . . this love is sooooooo encompassing.

I got to coach a young woman giving birth once . . . what an incredibly natural high it was to be present at this birth. I learned in an indelible way that the HOLY is most definitely WITHIN us. I discovered the INCARNATE God. There is nothing like holding a newborn to KNOW that we are all made in the image and likeness of God.

As I watched my daughter give birth to my granddaughter, words can't begin to describe it, but time stood still. During the process I relived giving birth to my daughter, and then suddenly here she is, a woman giving birth herself. Time ceased to be linear, yet I had a powerful sense of my own lineage: my great-grandmother, grandmother, mother, me, and my daughter. And here is my granddaughter, born with all her eggs, my future great-granddaughter. I felt an incredible connection to other women and was struck with the power that we women have, this biological connectedness, this fetus within a fetus, on down through the centuries the ability to give life. I felt strong and powerful as a woman—very, very feminine, with a sense of the spiritualness of femininity.

When my granddaughter opened her eyes, I knew I would protect her life with my own, if need be; she was just as much mine as my daughter's, I think, because we're all women, all of the oldest children going back several generations. Just holding her in my arms, I felt like all the trials and tribulations of raising a child were worth it just to have this moment with my grandchild. It's what life's all about: giving life and renewing it through the generations.

What I've learned from my maternal grandmother is the value of the grandparent relationship, and we work very hard to foster that with our children, who are lucky to have both sets of grandparents. What a powerful force they are in my children's lives, their wisdom and love and their ability to spoil children in ways unlike parents. I watch my children with their grandparents and long for the days of doing my grandma's hair or pulling the skin on the back of her hands or sitting on her lap and hearing about the "olden days."

Your first selfless act as a new mom is to give your child his/her "birth" day. While for me, my sons' births were two of the most precious days of my life, soon they became events for my children's pleasure and enjoyment. My sons are showered with gifts and attention, and I smile with a wonderful memory and warm gratitude. It's good to remember your own women friends on their child's birthday with a card, flower, or greeting as a reminder of the miracle they carried, cared for, and are now crazily running around trying to find matching napkins and party favors for.

MODELS FROM THE TRADITION

When we look to the saints and others for models of new life and the incarnational aspect of mothers' spirituality, three examples that emerge are St. Helena, St. Hildegard of Bingen, and Mother Teresa of Calcutta.

St. Helena (c. 250–330) was the mother of one of the most highly influential rulers of the ancient world, the emperor Constantine. Her conversion to Christianity, because of her position and wealth, had a strong impact on her era. According to ancient historians Helena led the search for one of the most important relics ever: the cross on which Jesus died—which had since been covered over by a temple to Aphrodite. She helped verify which one of the three crosses that were found was that of Jesus by its power to cure a dying woman when it touched her. Helena was also influential in the building of many ancient churches.

Her strong faith and influence points up a role for mothers everywhere: We are usually the ones who help preserve the tradition, the ones who keep the albums, the family trees and many of the family memories. We help all of us in remembering who we are and where we came from.

St. Hildegard of Bingen (1098–1179) is a remarkable woman in any century and even more so in her own time.

After having been raised and educated largely by an anchoress, a hermit living next to an abbey, she entered the monastic community and, later, became abbess upon her mentor's death. Not only did she have visions, which she later wrote about as well as writing other works of theology, but she also wrote excellent music and poetry, books about healing and herbs, and she was also a prophet and a preacher. An appreciative audience has recently rediscovered her.

Toward the end of her life Hildegard faced a challenging situation of inclusion; she allowed a young man who had been excommunicated by the church to be buried in the monastery cemetery. And when she was told to have the body removed, she refused because she understood that he had been reconciled with the church before dying. As a result of her refusal, the bishop placed her convent under sanctions that included no reception of the Eucharist, a condition that was eventually lifted.

Besides the importance of mercy to outsiders, Hildegard's life also reminds us of the holistic nature of women's concerns and the versatility that is often a part of the role of mother. Mothers are often called to be repair person, medical technician, chauffeur, as well as counselor and more—all in the course of an average day.

Mother Teresa of Calcutta (1910–1997) was an impressive example in our own day of caring for the *whole* person, especially those most left out in our society. Although she was trained as a Loreto nun and taught in India for over twenty years, this woman of Albanian extraction felt called to work with the poorest of the poor, starting with those dying on the streets of Calcutta.

She eventually helped those who joined the Missionaries of Charity, the order of nuns she founded, and many others to find and love Christ "in his most distressing disguise" in the sick, the dying, and the homeless. When she was later "discovered" by the world and given many awards and prizes, such as the Nobel Peace Prize in 1979, she was asked about how others could help in her impressive work. In response, she would often send people home to care tenderly for those close to them, especially someone hard to love, unwanted, or rejected. "Find your own Calcutta," she would say; do "something beautiful for God."

Mother Teresa challenges mothers to be the "incarnation" of God's love to those around us, in the unique way that only each of us can.

SCRIPTURE FOR REFLECTION

As we reflect on our own lives as mothers and the experience of new life and of the holistic dimension to our spirituality, the following passages may be helpful. Please try to take some time with one or more of these passages and with the questions following them. You may prefer to reflect on these with other mothers.

While they were [in Bethlehem], the time came for her to deliver her child.

And she gave birth to her firstborn son and wrapped him in bands of cloth, and laid him in a manger, because there was no place for them in the inn. In that region there were shepherds living in the fields, keeping watch over their flock by night. Then an angel of the Lord stood before them, and the glory of the Lord shone around them, and they were terrified. But the angel said to them, "Do not be afraid; for see—I am bringing you good news of great joy for all the people: to you is born this day in the city of David a Savior, who is the Messiah, the Lord. This will be a sign for you: you will find a child wrapped in bands of cloth and lying in a manger." And suddenly there was with the angel a multitude of the heavenly host, praising God and saying, "Glory to God in the highest heaven, and on earth peace among those whom he favors!" When the angels had left them and gone into heaven, the shepherds said to one another, "Let us go now to Bethlehem and see this thing that has taken place, which the Lord has made known to us." So they went with haste and found Mary and Joseph, and the child lying in the manger. When they saw this, they made known what had been told them about this child; and all who heard it were amazed at what the shepherds told them. But Mary treasured all these words and pondered them in her heart. (Luke 2:6–19)

—*What sights, smells, and sounds can you imagine in this scene?*
—*What may have been some of Mary's feelings at this time? How are they like what you have felt at times in your life?*
—*What experiences in your life have you "reflected on in your heart"?*

Now there was a man in Jerusalem whose name was Simeon; this man was righteous and devout, looking forward to the consolation of Israel, and the Holy Spirit rested on him. It had been revealed to him by the Holy Spirit that he would not see death before he had seen the Lord's Messiah.

Guided by the Spirit, Simeon came into the temple; and when the parents brought in the child Jesus, to do for him what was customary under the law, Simeon took him in his arms and praised God, saying, "Master, now you are dismissing your servant in peace, according to your word; for my eyes have seen your salvation, which you have prepared in the presence of all peoples, a light for revelation to the Gentiles and for glory to your people Israel." And the child's father and mother were amazed at what was being said about him. Then Simeon blessed them and said to his mother Mary, "This child is destined for the falling and the rising of many in Israel, and to be a sign that will be opposed so that the inner thoughts of many will be revealed—and a sword will pierce your own soul too."

There was also a prophet, Anna the daughter of Phanuel, of the tribe of Asher. She was of a great age, having lived with her husband seven years after her marriage, then as a widow to the age of eighty-four. She never left the temple but worshiped there with fasting and prayer night and day. At that moment she came, and began to praise God and to speak about the child to all who were looking for the redemption of Jerusalem. (Luke 2:25–38)

—*How do you picture the look on Simeon and Anna's faces as they saw the infant Jesus?*

—*Has anyone ever told you something about your child that surprised or amazed you?*

—*What older people of faith and wisdom have there been in your life or that of your child(ren)?*

[The king of Egypt] said to his people, "Look, the Israelite people are more numerous and more powerful than we. Come, let us deal shrewdly with them, or they will increase and, in the event of war, join our enemies and fight against us and escape from the land." Therefore they set taskmasters over them to oppress them with forced labor. They built supply cities, Pithom and Rameses, for Pharaoh. But the more they were oppressed, the more they multiplied and spread, so that the Egyptians came to dread the Israelites. The Egyptians became ruthless in imposing tasks on the Israelites, and made their lives bitter with hard service in mortar and brick and in every kind of field labor. They were ruthless in all the tasks that they imposed on them.

The king of Egypt said to the Hebrew midwives, one of whom was named Shiphrah and the other Puah, "When you act as midwives to the Hebrew women, and see them on the birthstool, if it is a boy, kill him; but if it is a girl, she shall live." But the midwives feared God; they did not do as the king of Egypt commanded them, but they let the boys live. So the king of Egypt summoned the midwives and said to them, "Why have you done this, and allowed the boys to live?" The midwives said to Pharaoh, "Because the Hebrew women are not like the Egyptian women; for they are vigorous and give birth before the midwife comes to them." So God dealt well with the midwives; and the people multiplied and became very strong.

And because the midwives feared God, he gave them families. (Exodus 1:9–21)

—*Have you ever faced a situation where you needed to act in conscience against what you were told to do? What helped you make that decision?*
—*When have you seen the strength and respect for life that Shiprah and Puah showed in yourself or in someone else?*

Other Scripture Passages to Explore
Exodus 1:22–2:10—The story of Moses being "adopted" by Pharaoh's daughter while his sister and mother also nurtured him.

2 Timothy 1:1–5—St. Paul recognizes the important role of Timothy's mother and grandmother in nurturing the young disciple's faith.

Questions for Individual or Group Reflection
What have been your experiences of birth? How did they help you to appreciate God more?

What experiences have helped you notice the holistic connections between your physical, mental, emotional, and spiritual health and well-being?

What is the holiest place in your home? Why? Would others in your family have a different answer?

What special objects from your family's past do you treasure, and what are the stories that accompany them?

What has been your experience of grandparents, especially grandmothers?

Resources for This Season
The following are some resources related to the themes explored here; full information on these can be found at the end of this book.

Coffey, *Immersed in the Sacred*
Finley, *Savoring God*
Houselander, *A Child in Winter*
Vivas, *The Nativity*
Zukerman, *In My Mother's Closet*

Chapter Three

LENT

The Disciplines of Motherhood

LIZ DIDN'T PARTICULARLY LIKE THE CHOICE SHE WAS facing. She needed some better clothes for job hunting, especially now that Bert, her husband, had lost his job. But the kids really needed clothes and supplies for the school year that was starting soon, and that couldn't wait. As she thought and prayed about what to do, she decided that maybe she could borrow something to wear from her friend, Maria—something that could tide her over until she or Bert found a job that could get them back on their feet financially.

Mothers face choices like Liz's fairly often, although the specifics may vary; those choices often entail caring for their families' needs at the cost, at least temporarily, of their own needs. Most of the time mothers will honor others' needs without thinking twice, but that doesn't mean it's always an easy choice to make.

WHAT IS THIS SEASON?

Self-examination and self-denial, part of what led Liz to her decision, are at the heart of the season of Lent, the forty days of preparation before the feast of Easter. In effect, it's a forty-day retreat—especially for adults preparing for Baptism. But it's also a kind of "continuing education" for the rest of us in the Christian community, a time to reflect on how well we are living out our call to follow Jesus.

The name "Lent" comes from the Anglo-Saxon word for spring and the lengthening of days that begins to be apparent at this time of year. From the earliest times the key feast of the Christian year was Easter. In order to prepare to celebrate it well, believers would at first fast for a couple days, which gradually became forty days by the fourth century. Forty—like the forty days that Noah and the others waited after the flood, like the forty years that the Israelites wandered in the desert after leaving Egypt, and—perhaps most importantly—like the forty days that Jesus spent in the desert after being baptized by John in the Jordan river.

As Jesus took time to do in the desert, all Christians need to explore for themselves what it means for *them* to be beloved of God, as Jesus knew he was at his baptism. And like Jesus, we need to confront the negative messages around us that tell us there are easier ways to live than to choose to love God and one another.

We are constantly being tempted and told that we don't have to deal with whatever pain we experience in growing up and living an authentic life, because there's probably a pill for whatever troubles us, whether it's physical pain, depression, or excess weight. And if all else fails, we can distract ourselves with some entertainment or food or just go shopping!

In the midst of a culture that encourages us to be as comfortable as possible, the themes of Lent are subtle and rather radical ones. But when we listen seriously to Jesus' message as he returned from the desert—his call to his listeners to re-form their lives—then taking some time to examine what's really important to us, and what we are choosing with our lives, looks more and more worthwhile.

Because our lives are deeply linked to others, mothers know that there are many times when our love will stretch us in ways we would rather not be stretched, but we also wouldn't have it any other way. There is a discipline, a kind of basic training that happens in a mother's experience, that teaches her—as a disciple—the deeper ways of the heart. This process of conversion and growth, however, is far from comfortable at times.

Three particular disciplines on which the Church focuses during Lent are prayer, fasting, and almsgiving. Prayer we will examine later when we look at the season of Ordinary Time, but let us explore the other two briefly and ponder their implications for mothers.

Fasting as a spiritual discipline is used by many religious traditions; it invites us to alter our eating or other habits temporarily as a way of putting our usual life "on hold" so that we can examine what really "nourishes" us. Fasting like this can have a cleansing effect on both body and mind. It's not the same as dieting because instead of focusing on looking good or feeding the ego—which can be a factor in weight watching—the emphasis is on emptying ourselves so that we can look around us to see "the bigger picture" in faith.

For example, if I decide not to have my usual morning cup of coffee, that may help me to be more intentional about what I'm doing in the morning and think about why I do what I do and about how I treat others. It also might lead me to think about the people growing and harvesting the coffee, about what I am supporting by what I buy and consume, and about those who may be going hungry. Or, instead of food, I might want to "fast" from a habit that I've become aware of, perhaps nagging a particular child too often or always having the last word in a conversation.

The key to whatever fasting I undertake is to allow the emptying to open me up. If, on the other hand, I'm constantly focusing on what I'm missing while I fast, I've missed the opportunity for a greater freedom to which fasting invites all of us. This freedom can be so important to mothers because we can easily fall into patterns that we may not like without even realizing it.

The discipline of *almsgiving* challenges us to share what we have been given more freely than we might otherwise. This may well involve giving money to the poor—perhaps saved from a simple meal one night a week during Lent— but it may also involve giving food to a local food bank or spending some time with someone who needs a caring presence. Perhaps for a family it might mean spending time talking to and just being with one another, instead of watching television or playing video games as usual.

The disciplines of Lent—prayer, fasting, and almsgiving—challenge us to look again at—to *re-spect*— ourselves and our choices, to see everything as a gift, and to consider other ways of using these gifts to share them more fully with others.

FROM THE TRADITION

What practices from the Christian tradition can be helpful to mothers in the self-examination to which Lent invites us?

Before Lent begins on Ash Wednesday, some cultures have a big celebration, a blowout party, prior to settling down to the forty somber days. This practice was especially strong in medieval times when the fast was much more severe and when no meat or fats of any kind were allowed during Lent.

The day before Ash Wednesday became known as Shrove Tuesday, just before people were *shriven* (forgiven after confession) from their sins, or it was called Fat Tuesday—in French *Mardi Gras*—because after that day no fat could be part of the diet until Easter. We have the remains of this time of celebration in places like Rio de Janeiro and New Orleans, times of *carnival*—literally, in Latin, a time for "farewell to meat."

For Fat Tuesday some families have pancakes or even doughnuts for dinner—silly foods perhaps, but traditional ones that once used up the fat in the cupboard. Others may dress up at this time of year as at Halloween, a good way to not take themselves too seriously.

Mothers today need to relearn the importance of celebration and silliness in our lives—and to help our families understand a playfulness that doesn't need a trip to the pizza parlor or game arcade to have fun. Can we have a simple party for Mardi Gras—or anytime—without having to buy coordinated plates and napkins? Younger children and other ethnic cultures can often be our teachers here, showing us how to slow down and celebrate. God created us with the wonderful ability to laugh; it's easy to take ourselves too seriously. Why not pull out some bubbles or some silly hats and find something to celebrate?

Ash Wednesday officially begins the season of Lent, with its vivid reminder that without God's gift of life and grace, all we are is dust. As the blessed ashes are applied to our foreheads, we may hear, "Remember that you are dust and to dust you shall return." A somber message indeed, but also one that reminds us of our ties to the earth.

In the second—and earlier—creation account in the book of Genesis, we read, ". . . the LORD God formed man out of the clay of the ground and blew into his nostrils the breath of life, and so man became a living being" (Genesis 2:7). This statement is profound; in a sense, it tells us that we're mud that breathes—not bad from a scientific standpoint, by the way, because we *are* made of the same hydrocarbons as the soil.

Scripture scholars tell us that the Hebrew word translated here as "man" is more properly a "human" or even an "earth creature," because this *adam* has come from the *adamah*, the earth. (Later in this same account, in a similar way the *ish* [male] and *ishshah* [female] will be closely linked as they are differentiated from one another, but not yet.) The connection Genesis suggests between the earth and being human may help explain why for many people—including a great number of women and mothers—gardening and being close to nature is helpful to their spirituality; they seem to feel more complete when close to the soil.

Yes, we *are* dust and to dust we shall return, and the difference between us and a lump of dirt in the Hebrew mind is *ruah*—here translated as "breath," but which also means wind and spirit. God's Spirit has given each of us the breath of life, the ability both to breathe and to love. And Ash Wednesday reminds us of what a gift that Spirit is for our very existence.

As Lent begins, besides receiving ashes at Church on Ash Wednesday, some families like to have a time of prayer together at home where they can write on slips of paper something for which they are sorry or something for which they wish to pray during this season. After these slips of paper have been collected and safely burned, they can sign each other's foreheads with the ashes. Other families may decorate a sign with the word "Alleluia," Hebrew for "praise God," and then put the sign in a box, which is buried or hidden, because this word won't be used again until Easter.

Ash Wednesday reminds mothers of what is really important—and what's not. Keeping the house clean, for example, just doesn't begin to compare to telling our children that we love them and helping them to know how special they are. And so much of what we spend our days worrying and stressing about doesn't *really* matter in light of the radical reevaluation to which Ash Wednesday invites us.

In a parish community a key focus during Lent is those who are becoming Catholic Christians through the **RCIA**, the Rite of Christian Initiation of Adults. This is a fairly recent revival of the ancient process of bringing new Christians into the Church. Those wishing to become Catholic who have never been baptized are called *catechumens*, while those who have been previously baptized in another Christian denomination are referred to as *candidates*, to honor the dignity of the baptism they have already received.

After an initial process of inquiry, both catechumens and candidates will receive months of education and formation, special times of blessings and prayers on the part of the whole parish community, as well as the support of their individual sponsors helping them through this process. All this finally culminates in the reception of Eucharist and Confirmation at the Easter Vigil on Holy Saturday, after Baptism for the catechumens and a profession of faith for the candidates. The community into which these new Christians and Catholics have come now receives them and celebrates with them the new life they have begun.

The RCIA reminds mothers that *any* formation is a gradual process in our lives and one that involves the whole community surrounding us. As mothers we are certainly important teachers for our children, but so are many others who affect them in ways we can't fully direct, even if we wanted to! The RCIA also reminds us of the importance of continuing to grow in, and learn about the gift of, our faith and our spirituality, because whatever isn't growing soon begins to die.

During the season of Lent, **special foods** may also help remind us of what this season is about. Some families serve **hot cross buns**, either just as Lent is beginning or as it draws to a close, as a reminder of Jesus' death on the cross.

Other homes have **pretzels** at each evening meal during Lent as a sign that this is a season of prayer. For many centuries these simple breads—made without milk or fat due to the fast but with a bit of salt for flavor—were a reminder to people to pray. The twined shape resembled both arms crossed with hands on shoulders, which was an early posture of prayer. The original name, *bracellae* ("little arms" in Latin) eventually became the pretzel name we know today.

These foods, and other special foods throughout the year, can be a good reminder that what we eat *does* affect who we are and that food can help build a deeper awareness of what we are "feeding" ourselves and our families in all kindsof ways. Food *is* an important part of the incarnational spirituality of mothers; next we explore another key quality.

MOTHERS' SPIRITUALITY IS *NURTURING*

Caring for others is a major focus during the season of Lent, and this is territory that moms know very well. Ever since we were little girls playing with dolls, most of us have been encouraged to nurture others and to focus on others and their needs. Whether it's caring for plants in the garden, cuddling a cute puppy or kitten, or babysitting from a fairly early age, most women and mothers have tended to notice and intuitively support the least ones, the children, and those left out.

Mothers often help out wherever we are; much of what we do without thinking twice for a neighbor in need—bringing a meal when someone is sick or has experienced a loss—is caring and almsgiving at work.

In fact, this tendency is so instinctive for most mothers that they are often amazed when they stop to consider how ingrained it is. When we stop to examine it, the focus on care and nurture in our spirituality as mothers has some understandable sources in our experience. Those of us who were pregnant have experienced the gradual separation from what was once a part of us, as Carol Ochs describes well in *Women and Spirituality*:

> The fetus, in utero, is both the self and the other. The mother identifies with it and yet is aware that its sleep pattern may not coincide with her own. In fact, often when the mother is still, preparing to sleep, the fetus is most active, forcing on the mother's awareness a realization of its otherness. During all the stages of childhood, there is the curious tension between deep identification with the child and growing awareness of its separateness and otherness. (p. 68)

Those mothers who have not experienced pregnancy also know the experience of deep caring, a caring that Elizabeth Stone describes this way: "Making the decision to have a child—it's momentous. It is to decide forever to have your heart go walking around outside your body."

Ochs also talks about two motions to motherhood: holding and letting go. Holding, for her, involves not only the literal, physical embrace of children, but also protecting them from physical harm by trying to foresee and prevent any dangers, being aware of the sensitivities of particular children, helping shape the way that the world is mediated to our children from their first hours, and establishing and maintaining a routine for children.

This complex set of caring, holding skills which she describes, however, not only will be different for each child but also begins to change as each child grows and changes, which brings us to the process of letting go, which we'll explore later in this chapter.

ACHIEVING A BALANCE

The nurture and care in which we are involved as mothers is complex indeed. How might this caring get out of balance at times?

On the one hand, as mothers we can tend to *care too much*. We are often sure that we know exactly what is best for our children—or others—and how they should get there. This smothering impulse is something all mothers need to watch for; in our "other-directed" love there is more of ourselves at times than we might want to admit. We know, for example, that the attentive care that a newborn needs can become counterproductive if maintained too long, not allowing a child to explore and learn about new possibilities.

Related to this tendency is *worrying too much* about our children or trying to control them, especially as they start to grow toward adulthood. One of the best gifts we can give our children, and at times one of the hardest to give, is that of trusting in their abilities and judgment.

Another way mothers can be out of balance when it comes to caring is to be *too concerned about what others think* and how they are feeling, whether the other person is a member of our family or not. Whenever we base our contentment and happiness on how others are doing, we are in the realm of codependency. Mothers can too easily live to try to please

others and keep them happy—even to the extreme of tolerating abusive behavior. Too many moms have stayed in abusive or unhealthy situations out of a misplaced desire to keep
things constant for their children, when in fact it probably
wasn't healthy for the kids, either. Mothers need to be wary
of an overemphasis on sacrifice in our spirituality.

Perhaps the most common imbalance for mothers is
caring for others so much that we forget to replenish ourselves. One
woman told me that when she hit a tough place in her life,
she realized that she could tell what each of her kids and her
ex-husband liked, but she couldn't even begin to tell what *she*
liked. She actually had to start with what she was sure she
didn't like and proceed from there!

This is so common among mothers that I consider it *the*
biggest challenge for our spirituality. If our own needs have
even made it onto our "to-do" list at all, they're usually toward
the bottom of it—and we never seem to get that far down on
the list! We tend to forget that we are told—commanded—by
Jesus to love our neighbor *as ourselves*, which means that our
care of others is built upon a healthy love for ourselves.

The way I first began to learn this lesson was quite literal and physical. I was trying to breast-feed our newborn
oldest son *and* do everything I had previously expected of
myself. I began to quickly see that if I didn't rest enough and
drink enough fluids, *there would be literally nothing left to give.*
Around that time I found that I became far more aware of
whether friends of mine were taking good enough care of
themselves in order not to "burn out."

When mothers *can* balance their caring energies well—
not caring too much and remembering to replenish themselves in a healthy and balanced way—they can be strong and
healthy sources of the loving care our world so badly needs.

BREAST-FEEDING: A NOURISHING LOVE

A powerful experience of nurturing available to many mothers of newborns is that of nursing their children. For some women the experience of breast-feeding has been an important part of their motherhood—and their spirituality. Theologian Wendy Wright describes her experience this way in her book *Sacred Dwelling*:

> To nurse a child is to do so much more than simply to give nourishment. It is not only a means by which our species assures the physical survival of its young. To nurse a child is to enter into a complex, almost symbiotic, relationship with another human being. In nursing one learns two arts suited for the cultivation of the spiritual life: the art of attentiveness and the art of giving from one's own substance. (p. 105)

She sees this attentiveness as the opportunity to appreciate up close the unique mystery of each particular child and then to give that child in a very real sense a part of oneself.

Margaret Hebblethwaite describes her experience at times of a deep sense of God's presence and of prayer as she fed her child:

> In those times I prayed. As I held my baby in stillness and quiet, it was a perfect time to turn to God. "I have calmed and quieted my soul, like a child quieted at its mother's breast; like a child that is quieted is my soul" (Psalms 131:2). I would look at my baby and reflect: "I'm holding you, and God's holding me. I'm feeding you, and God's feeding me." It was at these moments of prayer that I began to perceive God as the source of all motherly love, giving me the warmth, safety, and nourishment I needed to hand on to my child. (p. 11)

Of course, both women would quickly add that not every experience of nursing one's child is nearly this prayerful; there are many times when other pressures intrude or the very routineness of it tends to dull our sensitivities. And women who choose not to, or are unable to, breast-feed have had other similar times that call them to stop and nourish this child—and themselves.

Every time we feed our children—or change their diapers or give them a ride or cheer them on or listen to their concerns—we are a powerful sign to them of God's faithful, nurturing love. And we are presented with yet another opportunity to see that our nurturing love for our children is just a tiny glimpse of God's tender and endless love for us.

A Mother's Influence: Another Look at Mary

As our children continue to grow and as we try to love them, what can we say about the daily experience of being a mother? What about all the times when it can feel that, if our love is a sign of God's love, it's an extremely imperfect sign? Much of what we do for our children each day is hidden from view, just as Mary's daily experience and her influence is not discussed much at all in the New Testament.

Apart from the incident of finding the twelve-year-old Jesus in the temple, which is related in Luke's gospel, we don't know anything more about Jesus or Mary until the beginning of Jesus' public life, except that they lived in Nazareth. All we are told is that "The child grew and became strong, filled with wisdom; and the favor of God was upon him" (Luke 2:40), and later: "Jesus advanced (in) wisdom and age and favor before God and man" (Luke 2:52).

We are also told that ". . . his mother kept all these things in her heart" (Luke 2:51), a phrase we also hear about Mary after the visit of the shepherds.

What happened during those years for Mary and Jesus? And what happens for *us* during those years we are helping our children cope with everything from losing a tooth to losing a game or a friend? A video, called *Mary, Mother of Jesus* (1999), written by Albert Ross and based on material by John Goldsmith, suggests some interesting possibilities about Mary's influence as a mother—and our own influence as mothers.

Did Mary tell the child Jesus stories at bedtime, like the one about the Good Samaritan, that he later used when he was teaching people? Did she teach him about the Jewish scriptures, which helped give him the impressive knowledge he showed when he was with the teachers in the Temple? Did John the Baptist also baptize her in the Jordan, right after Jesus? And was she Jesus' confidante, supporting him as he was trying to understand what he was called to by God—much as she herself had struggled to follow God's call? The video suggests that she may have been influential in these ways, helping shape Jesus' teachings and ministry more than we may think; we'll never know for sure.

And we will also never fully know the influence *we* have as mothers on our children and on others around us. We *do* know that we teach far more by what we *do* than by what we say, by our *example* than by our giving our children "The Look" or by lecturing them. We are teaching them about people skills, about taking risks, about the value of serving others, about the importance of imagination, and about work skills and how to handle leisure time—more than we have any idea.

Although we *don't* completely know our impact on our children, we *can* ask God for insight and wisdom and the gifts to teach them what they need to learn from us, knowing that God is the ultimate teacher for all of us.

LETTING GO:
THE PAIN OF MOTHERS

Knowing that our God *is* there for our children, in ways that we can never be, can help us when it comes to the challenge of gradually letting go of our children, but it still doesn't make that process easy. Letting go is something we can't escape as mothers, no matter how hard we try; our children start leaving us from the moment they're born. In a sense, to sign on as a parent is to sign on to more "goodbyes" than "hellos."

Being a mother involves a careful dance between holding on and letting go, between protecting our children and yet letting them experience the consequences of their actions—and at times many of us don't feel like very graceful dancers! A major complication is that each of our children has different "steps" to their "choreography" and unique challenges to how and when to let them go.

Our middle son, for example, has always seemed to have a very strong sense of independence. Once when he was about four, he was headed out the back door to play, and I asked him to get a jacket because it was cold outside. No, he was just fine. After several unsuccessful tries at getting him to wear a jacket, I mentioned that his fly was unzipped, too. As he reached down to zip it up, he boldly declared, "I'm a lot warmer now!"

Letting go is much more than whether to have a preschooler wear a jacket, of course. We start practicing this long process as mothers right away, when we're not able to control the way our bodies work during pregnancy or the timing of labor and the birth itself or the process of adoption. Then there's the challenge of the sleeping and eating schedule of each infant, of the toddler's next new accomplishment—including potty training. Then it's starting school, learning to ride a bike, and so many new skills, and then adolescence and beyond.

And as our children grow further, we need to let go further as they learn to drive, graduate, and leave home for college or a job, marriage, and even the first grandchild. In between there are plenty of other "practice" opportunities: going to various lessons, watching them winning and losing games, going to camp and other travel, perhaps making some big mistakes and even having legal trouble—as well as accidents or illnesses.

At the end of his seventh grade year, the same middle son I mentioned earlier was the only person with any serious injuries in a two-car collision near our home. We raced to the scene when we got a call about what had happened, only to watch the emergency personnel prying him out of the car with what they call the "jaws of life."

He was in the hospital for a week, at least half of that time in intensive care. He was lucky to have had only internal injuries but there was also some amount of impact to his head—we didn't know how much. He would drift in and out of consciousness, while everyone we knew was praying for him.

We all had to let go of what would happen to him, knowing he was in God's hands. We always are in God's care, of course, but we are far more aware of that reality when times of crisis come. (Thankfully, he was able to make an amazing recovery and was back in school within a week, even playing in a basketball tournament within the month!)

I believe that each of our children is first of all God's child, just on loan to us. As they grow older we increasingly need to give them back to God and say, "They're in Your hands now more than mine; I've done the best I could. Please be with them, now that I can't be there all the time any longer." Sometimes we *know* that we needed to turn them back over to God; at other times we need friends to *remind us* of the fact that it isn't all up to us—even when we think it is.

Perhaps one of the biggest experiences of letting go for mothers is that of letting go of the mother we thought we could be. In *Motherhood: A Spiritual Journey*, Ellyn Sanna talks about the experience of realizing that one is not the Perfect Mother:

> When we experience failure in our motherhood, then we are not being torn from our children, but from our own egos, from the self-centered identities we have clung to all our lives . . . hurt and frustration are givens in the mother–child dyad, just as they are in any human relationship. No matter how much we love each other, sooner or later we all hurt one another.
>
> We all fail our children, just as our parents all failed us, just as our children will one day fail their children. The experience is an age-old cycle. We'd like to be immune from the wheel of pain. We'd like to think we know more than our own mothers did or that we love our children more or that our level of understanding is somehow greater, that for whatever reason we won't make the same mistakes our mothers did. But we will. In one way or another, we wound our children. (pp. 100–101)

She explains that unless we *do* fail our children in some way or other, there would be no reason for them to separate from us and become independent individuals. And they would not realize their own need for God if we supplied all their needs. So it is out of our own weakness and pain that God brings gifts for growth—for our children and for us.

RECONCILIATION: SACRAMENT OF FORGIVENESS

Mothers know only too well the experience of weakness and pain—in themselves and their children—and they long for the forgiveness and healing that is celebrated in the sacrament of Reconciliation.

The early Christians realized fairly soon that they needed a way to ritualize and celebrate the forgiving love that Jesus taught and lived, a love stronger and deeper than any wrong choices they could make. Human failings and sinfulness were coming to light in their communities, and they needed a way to be able to reintegrate those who had made these mistakes back into the community of believers, especially after serious problems like murder, apostasy (renouncing one's faith under threat of punishment), and adultery.

This sacrament took many forms in various places in the early centuries, but it often involved a three-year public process, occurring only once in a lifetime, where the penitent wore sackcloth and was sprinkled with ashes—ashes which later began to be used for the whole community on Ash Wednesday.

In the Celtic countries of Ireland and England, meanwhile, another tradition gradually emerged, which was more private and frequent, like the practice of spiritual direction, which also originated there. Gradually, by the medieval period this Celtic approach to individual confession had become more widespread, and the other approach had basically died out.

As a result, the theology of this sacrament that emerged tended to emphasize a fourfold process of reconciliation: contrition, confession, absolution, and satisfaction. The new rite of the sacrament of Reconciliation in the Catholic Church, since 1973, reemphasizes the communal aspect of reconciliation and integrates a more prayerful and scriptural approach.

Forgiveness and reconciliation are a frequent part of a mother's world and of what she teaches to her children. For example, she can help a child learn the distinction between his breaking something accidentally and his meaning to cause some harm, the importance of taking responsibility for what he did and yet the difference between appropriate guilt about something that he *did* and crippling shame about who he *is*, and the value of celebrating a reconciliation by doing something together after the wrongdoing has been admitted.

As mothers we have the opportunity to help our children appreciate that our love for them is stronger than anything they can do to "mess up." We try to love them with the kind of love God shows each of us: an unconditional, *as-is* love, not a conditional, *if-only* love. Just as *we* don't do a perfect job of any aspect of being a mother, even of forgiveness, neither are our children perfect.

The true challenge of forgiveness for all of us in our relationship with God is *not* that God has not forgiven us our failings, but that we have not forgiven *ourselves*. Once we can appreciate and accept God's healing care for us, it's just that much easier for us to forgive our children and others who may hurt us.

MOTHERS SPEAK

Again we hear from mothers and their experience as it reflects the themes of this Lenten season:

I wish someone had told me that my own love would not be enough . . . that I would need to lean heavily on God for love of the highest quality with my children. You feel so much love for a baby that it's hard to imagine ever not adoring him, but when those times do come, you need to understand that God's love for your child is greater than your own, untainted with selfishness, and can be infused into your own heart.

My teenaged son seemed to grow more obnoxious every day, and we were more and more at odds with each other over trivial things. I prayed, searched my heart for faults, tried every avenue of communication with him, to no avail. There seemed to be no responsiveness in him to love, to tenderness, to reason, or to religious precepts. It was growing harder and harder to love him as he daily rejected my love and seemed hell-bent to be as unlovable as possible.

Finally, I cried out to God for love of this child I could hardly recognize. I had reached the end of my own feelings for him and he was barricaded against receiving anything from me. I realized that his behavior was, among other things, his way of breaking what had been a very close connection between us so that he could go on to independence. I was able to focus all my love for him on the one mother–son offering left between us: folding his laundry.

For months, I folded those T-shirts and paired those socks, praying that he would receive it as a peace offering. My love for him grew as I served him in this tiny way. I began to include little love notes among the clean clothes and to encourage him in the new life he was starting as a college student. I focused on staying noncombative, no matter what buttons he pushed, and on doing this little thing (as Mother Teresa teaches) with great love.

He never said thanks, and when I would begin to feel hurt by that ingratitude, God reminded me that it was a gift given to me to be able to do this one thing for him in love. When he realized that I would not participate in his unconscious plan of creating a harsh break between us, he began to trust that I loved him without any strings that might tie him down, and when he finally left home, it was with peace between us.

Being a mother has been the hardest thing I've ever done, yet the most fulfilling. Being a mother keeps me humble and knowing how much I depend on God on a daily moment-by-moment basis. I've had to learn to let go, to surrender in so many ways. As a strong "SJ" on the Meyers-Briggs [personality test], I've had to learn to go with the flow, to be open to surprises, and to trust things will work out, even though 99.9 percent of the time it isn't in my timing or plans!

Kahlil Gibran has it right: our children are not our own. It has been a source of strength and comfort to me to recognize that they belong to God. Also, as a result of my work as a teacher, and seeing how damaging it can be when mothers (or fathers) try to fulfill their own wishes and needs and build their own egos through the lives of their children, I would say to mothers, be self-aware, check your motivations as you respond to the playing out of your children's lives. Respect that this is their life, not yours.

When my two children were older teenagers, one day in prayer a light bulb went on. I realized that even if I could direct my children's lives, just like a theater director directs a play, things would still get messed up and mistakes would happen, because I had been more or less in charge of my own life, and it certainly hadn't gone without mishap or mistake. . . . I also realized that I had much to learn from my children. My husband often said that our daughter got me for a mom because I was someone who had within me the patience and love to raise her, but I know just as well that God gave her to me because living with her and bringing her up was an opportunity for me to learn a lot.

Our four kids ranged from three to fifteen, and I don't know if I had unduly high expectations (like having someone say "Happy Mother's Day") or if they were just particularly ungrateful and obnoxious that day, but by midday I had had it and wrote my despair down in a letter to them. I don't remember if I actually showed it to them, but I do remember saying that I feared the oldest was headed toward being an ornery materialist, the second an irresponsible unwed mother, the third a maladjusted sociopath, and the fourth a reckless street bum.

That was a powerful experience, but the more powerful part is realizing that just a few years ago the ornery materialist was leading us around Indonesia, speaking the native language as he fulfilled a year of volunteer teaching. Then, just a few months ago, we had a similar experience with the second as she guided us around Mali in West Africa, where she is a Peace Corps volunteer for two years. She had been irresponsible enough to learn two African languages and live in a village without electricity or running water!

MODELS FROM THE TRADITION

When we look to the saints and others for models of letting go and of the nurturing aspect of mothers' spirituality, three examples that emerge are St. Catherine of Siena, Etty Hillesum, and four of the many martyrs killed in El Salvador.

St. Catherine of Siena (1347–1380) was a mystic who wrote eloquently about God's love and had many visions, but she also had to battle misunderstanding from her family and from many others as she led a life of prayer and serving the poor while living at home as a lay follower of St. Dominic. Her healing work among the poor and her own deep spirituality attracted many followers, who called themselves "the Caterinata." This group included men and women and some priests and friars, who called her Mamma.

One of her most impressive gifts was as a peacemaker, and she tried to help settle conflicts between the city of Florence and the pope, who had moved to Avignon, France, because of the political and military chaos around Rome. She spoke frankly to the pope, both in written form and later in person: He needed to be in Rome where his sheep awaited a shepherd. "Come then, come and delay no more; and comfort you and fear not for anything that might happen to you, since God will be with you" (quoted in Jones, p. 20). The pope eventually did return to Rome, in part because of her appeal.

Catherine reminds mothers of the determination and deep love that mothers possess, qualities that help them to continue to believe in their children and to have hope when things may look bleak.

Etty Hillesum (1914–1943) also lived at a very difficult time, but within the past century. She was a young Jewish woman living in Amsterdam during the Nazi occupation there; she later died in Auschwitz with so many others, including saints like Edith Stein and Maximilian Kolbe. The journals that she left behind were begun at about the same time as the better-known diary of Anne Frank, who was hiding not far away from where she lived. In the face of the Holocaust, of which she was clearly aware, she shows us a mysticism and an honest, deep love of God. She writes:

> I now realise, God, how much You have given me. So much that was beautiful and so much that was hard to bear. Yet whenever I showed myself ready to bear it, the hard was directly transformed into the beautiful. And the beautiful was sometimes much harder to bear, so overpowering did it

seem. To think that one small human heart can experience so much, oh God, so much suffering and so much love, I am so grateful to You, God for having chosen my heart, in these times, to experience all the things it has experienced. (*An Interrupted Life*, p. 207)

Although Etty had some opportunities to escape the fate of her fellow Jews, she felt she needed to be with them in their hope as well as in their suffering. From the window of the transport train headed to Poland she tossed out a card that read, "We have left the camp singing." She is a reminder of the ways that love makes *all* things possible, even deep suffering.

Like Catherine of Siena and Etty Hillesum, the four women who were martyred by military violence in El Salvador on December 2, 1980, were not biological mothers, but they were mothers of the heart. **Jean Donovan**, a lay woman, and **Sisters Maura Clarke**, **Ita Ford**, and **Dorothy Kazel**, all missionaries from the United States, had been working with the Salvadoran poor.

Sr. Ita Ford had written to her niece in the United States about how difficult life was for the young people her niece's age, but also how they seemed to have found a meaning in their lives worth living—and dying—for. She added:

> Brooklyn is not passing through the drama of El Salvador, but some things hold true wherever one is, and at whatever age. What I'm saying is that I hope you can come to find that which gives life a deep meaning for you, something that energizes you, enthuses you, enables you to keep moving ahead. (Ellsberg, p. 527)

Jean Donovan, the youngest of the group and who had been weighing some other career options, wrote home two weeks before her death, "Several times I have decided to leave—I almost could except for the children, the poor bruised victims of adult lunacy. Who would care for them? Whose heart would be so staunch as to favor the reasonable thing in a sea of their tears and loneliness? Not mine, dear friend, not mine" (p. 527).

Each of the four women had chosen to stay with the poor of El Salvador—a dangerous choice, they knew, especially in the light of the death nine months before of Archbishop Oscar Romero, who was a powerful spokesman for the poor of the country. In his words, quoted by Ita Ford the night before her death, "One who is committed to the poor must risk the same fate as the poor. And in El Salvador we know what the fate of the poor signifies: to disappear, to be tortured, to be captive, and to be found dead" (Ellsberg, p. 526). Unfortunately, this is exactly what these four women experienced.

While most mothers will not undergo what they did, these women martyrs from El Salvador remind us of what the choice to love can cost us at times.

SCRIPTURE FOR REFLECTION

As we reflect on our own lives as mothers and the disciplines within motherhood, including the experience of letting go and of the nurturing aspect to our spirituality, the following passages may be helpful. Please try to take some time with one or more of these passages and with the questions following them. You may prefer to reflect on these with other mothers.

Just then a lawyer stood up to test Jesus. "Teacher," he said, "what must I do to inherit eternal life?" He said to him, "What is written in the law? What do you read there?" He answered, "You shall love the Lord your God with all your heart, and with all your soul, and with all your strength, and with all your mind; and your neighbor as yourself." And he said to him, "You have given the right answer; do this, and you will live" (Luke 10:25–28).

—*How well do you do at loving others as yourself? Do you need to work further at loving yourself? How?*
—*How do you see a link between your love of God and love of others? Who has helped you understand this connection?*

Now every year [Jesus'] parents went to Jerusalem for the festival of the Passover. And when he was twelve years old, they went up as usual for the festival. When the festival was ended and they started to return, the boy Jesus stayed behind in Jerusalem, but his parents did not know it. Assuming that he was in the group of travelers, they went a day's journey. Then they started to look for him among their relatives and friends. When they did not find him, they returned to Jerusalem to search for him. After three days they found him in the temple, sitting among the teachers, listening to them and asking them questions. And all who heard him were amazed at his understanding and his answers. When his parents saw him they were astonished; and his mother said to him, "Child, why have you treated us like this? Look, your father and I have been searching for you in great anxiety."

He said to them, "Why were you searching for me? Did you not know that I must be in my Father's house?" But they did not understand what he said to them. Then he went down with them and came to Nazareth, and was obedient to them. His mother treasured all these things in her heart. (Luke 2:41–51)

—*Have you ever had to look for a child? Remember how that felt.*

—*How do your experiences of letting go intersect with the letting go that Mary and Joseph were called to here?*

—*How does your faith help you accept what you can't understand right now?*

Is not this the fast that I choose: to loose the bonds of injustice, to undo the thongs of the yoke, to let the oppressed go free, and to break every yoke?

Is it not to share your bread with the hungry, and bring the homeless poor into your house; when you see the naked, to cover them, and not to hide yourself from your own kin? Then your light shall break forth like the dawn, and your healing shall spring up quickly; your vindicator shall go before you, the glory of the LORD shall be your rear guard. Then you shall call, and the LORD will answer; you shall cry for help, and he will say, Here I am. If you remove the yoke from among you, the pointing of the finger, the speaking of evil, if you offer your food to the hungry and satisfy the needs of the afflicted, then your light shall rise in the darkness and your gloom be like the noonday.

The LORD will guide you continually, and satisfy your needs in parched places, and make your bones strong; and you shall be like a watered garden, like a spring of water, whose waters never fail. (Isaiah 58:6–11)

—*How do you share what you have with those around you? (Think again before answering this; you probably do so more than you think.)*

—*Who can you reach out to who could use your help while you balance this with a healthy love of self so that you are not taken advantage of?*

Other Scripture Passages to Explore
Matthew 18:21–35—Our forgiveness of one another—
more than seven times seventy—is based on God's forgiveness of us.

2 Maccabees 7:1–41—A strong mother supports her
seven sons' faith and refusal to abandon the Jewish law in the
face of persecution.

Questions for Individual or Group Reflection
How have you been "stretched" by love?

From what do you need to fast? When has fasting been helpful for you in the past?

How is being close to the earth part of your spirituality, if
it is? What—and who—has helped you grow in faith?

Where are your challenges in holding and letting go? How
have you been an important influence on your child(ren)?

How did you learn about forgiveness? How well can you forgive yourself?

Resources for This Season
*The following are some resources related to the themes explored here; full
information on these can be found at the end of this book.*

Brennan, *The Way of Forgiveness*
An Interrupted Life: The Diaries of Etty Hillesum 1941–43
Hebbelthwaite, *Motherhood and God*
Mary, the Mother of Jesus (video)
Ochs, *Women and Spirituality*
Wright, *Sacred Dwelling*

Chapter Four

HOLY WEEK AND EASTER
Dying and Rising

It was one of the hardest experiences of my life, a time of birth and of death. After two years of marriage my husband Mitch and I found ourselves pregnant, although our "plan" had been to wait another couple years until he had finished graduate school. Our initial surprise, however, had turned to delight, and the pregnancy seemed to be going well. I had just finished my job at a nearby parish the day before, and the staff there had given me a wonderful baby shower as I left.

But in the middle of the following night my water broke, and our world turned upside down, since the pregnancy was only about five months along. In retrospect, the baby had probably dropped a few days before that, but I didn't know what to expect with my first pregnancy.

We raced to the nearest hospital, although we'd practiced the way to another one, where we'd just begun childbirth classes. While Mitch drove, I was trying to breathe with the contractions, recalling what I had read and heard. A few blocks from the hospital we saw flashing lights behind us; we were being stopped for speeding at two a.m.! After we quickly explained the situation to the policeman, we were given an escort to the emergency room.

The hospital staff whisked me into a delivery room where the baby came quite quickly, and although they tried to use a breathing tube to get him to breathe, but he was just too small to make it. Our child, the one we had so excitedly awaited, was dead.

They kept me in the hospital overnight while poor Mitch went home to an empty apartment. I was sent home the next day and told to rest. We were numb, clinging to each other, crying in disbelief and pain.

WHAT IS THIS SEASON?

The death of a loved one—as we experienced—puts the gift, and the questions, of life in clear relief. Death and dying, life and living, all come to a dramatic climax in the final days of Lent, called Holy Week, and Easter.

From Passion Sunday on, the events at the end of Jesus' life rush by: the triumphant entry into Jerusalem, the final Passover meal with his followers, his night in the Garden of Gethsemane, the arrest and a sham trial, followed by torture and being forced to carry his own cross to the place of execution. And then after Jesus' death and burial comes the news of his resurrection from the dead, stunning his followers because it's too good to believe.

Originally these events were all commemorated in one feast, referred to as *Pascha*, a Christian Passover or Easter. In the fourth century the feasts were divided much as they are today and were celebrated in Jerusalem, on or near the places where the events had occurred, later spreading to the rest of the Christian world.

Holy Week begins with **Passion Sunday**, also called Palm Sunday. In church we hear the passion account from one of the gospels, usually while holding palms much like those the crowd may have been holding while cheering Jesus as a hero as he entered Jerusalem—only to be calling for his crucifixion a few days later. (Fittingly, the blessed palms not taken home on this day end up being burned the following year to make the ashes that are then used for Ash Wednesday.)

Like the fickle crowd and the apostle Peter—who swore his love and support for Jesus, only to deny him under pressure—we mothers watch ourselves and our children falter at times, when we're not consistent in our love and our choices. But we also hear Jesus' message of forgiveness and accepting love, a love which accepted Peter and which cares for us even when we fall short in our ability to love.

After Palm Sunday, the focus shifts to the last three days of the week, the most important part of the liturgical year and what is known as the Easter Triduum, Latin for "a space of three days": Holy Thursday, Good Friday, and the Easter Vigil on Holy Saturday.

Holy Thursday, also called Maundy Thursday because of the commandment (*mandatum* in Latin) to wash one another's feet mentioned in John's gospel, recalls the Last Supper and the institution of the sacrament of the Eucharist, which we will explore later in this season.

The liturgy for Holy Thursday is more festive than during the season of Lent, but the shadow of Jesus' impending arrest and crucifixion also hangs over this feast. Mothers know this bittersweet feeling when a time of celebration also marks an end to a relationship as we have known it, whether it's a graduation or a funeral or even a wedding. While we know in our hearts that change needs to happen, looking back and saying goodbye seems easier than facing an unclear or difficult future.

An optional ritual in the renewed liturgy for Holy Thursday is the washing of the feet, based on Jesus' actions as recorded in John's gospel. (See "Scripture for Reflection," this chapter.) This is far more than a pantomime of what Jesus did with his disciples in the upper room; it is an opportunity for a parish community to renew their commitment to serving others as Jesus did. Some families choose to do this at home with one another, washing one another's feet or hands. Whether at church or at home, this is a powerful sensory experience that says so much more than words can convey.

Mothers, of course, are involved in "washing others' feet"—and other parts of their bodies—every day, starting with infants' tiny toes and perhaps later trying to bring down a child's fever or even cleaning up after someone has been sick. It happens so often that we hardly give it a second thought, but it's good to remember that it is *Jesus* that we are serving in the least of his brothers and sisters, as he reminds us.

As the Holy Thursday liturgy ends, the Eucharist is taken away from the main altar and placed in a special place of adoration, and the altar is then stripped, because this is a grim, bare time, a time of sadness and reflection, of quiet waiting. Mothers know this waiting—up at night with a sick child or trying to find out the results from medical tests, chemo- or radiation therapy, or surgery for themselves or a friend or family member. The hours and days stretch on, and clocks and calendars cannot measure the waiting for us. All we are left with is prayer.

And then comes **Good Friday**—good in the sense of the love that it manifests—a time to recall Jesus' suffering and death, not in order to glorify suffering for its own sake, but to remember the cost that Love is willing to pay.

No Mass is celebrated on Good Friday; there is, rather, a Liturgy of the Word, including the Passion account from

John's gospel, followed by the Veneration of the Cross—a time for each person to come and kiss or touch the cross, the sign of Jesus' passion and death and a reminder of the cross we are each called to carry. Before the cross is venerated we hear three times, "This is the wood of the cross on which hung the Savior of the World." We are asked to do something that is quite radical in our culture: to look pain and death in the face instead of denying its existence or numbing it.

This cross and pain will take different shape in each of our lives and at different times; it may be emotional, relational, physical, or social. Emotional pain may involve relationships that aren't as healthy as they could be, disappointment about hopes and dreams that have never materialized, or, perhaps, depression or addiction. Relational pain can be found in an unhappy marriage, a divorce, or, perhaps, difficulties with family or friends. Physical pain may include illness, abuse, or disabilities. Social pain encompasses so much, including prejudice, poverty, and the many kinds of injustice. Whenever pain—of whatever kind—is part of our days, Jesus is there, suffering in us and around us in many ways; we remember that experience also when we celebrate Jesus' Passion.

The liturgy for Good Friday ends with a communion service, as hosts are distributed that were consecrated at Mass the previous day. The sad and somber tone of this time is heightened by its being a day of fasting and abstinence from meat. In the midst of our noise-saturated culture some families choose to emphasize the seriousness of the day by having no noise in the home between noon and three o'clock, the time during which Jesus traditionally hung on the cross.

In the face of the mystery of death—of Jesus or anyone—what can we say or do? Whether mothers have experienced the death of a loved one or not, they have lived with the death of hopes and dreams, with the reality of injustice, with a lost job or even the death of a pet. We stand speech-less before the pain, not knowing what to do or say, whether it is our own pain or that of someone close to us.

But Good Friday is not the end of the story, thankfully. In sadness, but with a hope the first disciples didn't yet have on the first Good Friday, we know that, although there is a body in Jesus' tomb, it won't be there for long. Our Christian hope tells us that with the death of the way we thought things would be comes a rebirth of new possibilities beyond our wildest dreams.

The liturgy for the Easter Vigil on **Holy Saturday** starts after sundown in a darkened church with the dramatic blessing of the new fire, from which tapers are lit among all those gathered, and bits of light begin to spread in the dark-ness, much like the light of faith, which is not dimmed as it is shared. Later in this very earthy and elemental liturgy, any catechumens or candidates studying to become Catholic will be baptized, confirmed, and welcomed into the church.

But first there is the blessing and lighting of the large Paschal candle, and its triumphant procession into church while we hear three times, "The Light of Christ," to which everyone responds, "Thanks be to God." Later in the liturgy this candle, a symbol of Christ and the traditionally male ele-ment of fire, may be plunged into the traditionally feminine element of water as it is blessed before being used for Baptism.

In the light of this candle we hear a series of readings from the Old and New Testaments, reminding us of the promise of salvation which now culminates in Jesus and his resurrection to new life, the Light in the midst of darkness. This condensed version of salvation history reminds us of the roots of what brings us together as a community. Just af-ter the gospel about the empty tomb is read, the worship space comes alive with light, our senses are filled with colors and flowers, and we hear bells and alleluias, sounds which have been missing for the past forty days. Death has not had the last word!

This is the time when those who have been preparing for months to come into the Church are now baptized, confirmed, and welcomed, and all those who are gathered also renew their own baptismal commitment and promises, as will those who come the next morning, on **Easter Sunday**, to celebrate the resurrection on the morning of the new day. But this is just the beginning; the Easter season is fifty days of celebration, culminating in Pentecost.

The days of the Easter Triduum—Holy Thursday, Good Friday, and Holy Saturday—put us at the heart of the *paschal mystery*, the dying and rising of Jesus—and the dying and rising to which we all are called, every day. The Jesuit theologian Karl Rahner called this experience "dying in installments."

As mothers we are called to die and rise in so many ways: to set aside most of our expectations for our children, to love them even while not liking their choices—or even our children themselves, at times—to serve in many ways that may never be noticed or appreciated, and to let go in the countless ways we explored in discussing the season of Lent. Mothers experience *plenty* of dying and, hopefully, also see the rising of new possibilities in themselves and in their children—even in the very dying to which they are called.

FROM THE TRADITION

What practices from the Christian tradition can help enhance our appreciation of the dying and rising to which Holy Week and Easter invite us?

The **Stations of the Cross**, or Way of the Cross, is a traditional devotion often used during Lent and the early part of Holy Week; it offers a way for Christians to imagine and "follow in Jesus' footsteps" through the experience of his passion and death. This practice had its origins in the travels of those who visited the sites in Jerusalem associated with Jesus' passion and death, especially during antiquity and the time of the Crusades.

For those who could not make this pilgrimage, shrines and representations were made that would help them imagine what Jesus had endured. These have varied widely in form and in number through the centuries, but eventually the number of stations was established at fourteen, and now they are found on the walls of most Catholic churches. Those who pray with these stations walk, if possible, from one station to another, reflecting on what happened to Jesus and the way in which Jesus continues to suffer in our world today.

The stations begin with Jesus being condemned to death by Pilate and include Jesus falling three times, his meeting his mother (the fourth station), the woman Veronica wiping the face of Jesus (the sixth station), and his meeting and speaking to the women of Jerusalem (the eighth station). The fourteenth station is that of Jesus being placed in the tomb. Modern liturgists have also encouraged the addition of a fifteenth station: that of the resurrection.

Mothers have their own stations of the cross—in all the ways they are called to die and rise that we have already mentioned. And, often even more difficult for them, they watch *their children* suffer and fall repeatedly, knowing that as mothers they can do little to help besides being present and praying, just as Mary did for Jesus.

A couple other traditions that are connected with Holy Week and Easter are far more positive and joyful: **spring cleaning** and the wearing of **new clothes at Easter**.

Cleaning and the paschal mystery may not seem to have anything in common at first, but a second look suggests at least a couple connections. The early part of Holy Week was a traditional time for a thorough housecleaning in the past, an opportunity to get rid of what was old and dusty from Winter and prepare for the new life of Spring, a practice which may even have had links to the Jewish custom of getting rid of the old yeast in preparation for the feast of the unleavened bread, Passover. And any cleaning, whether with modern conveniences or a simple broom, involves a kind of death and rebirth; first we seem to make a bigger mess before we get cleaner results—a little dying and rising many times a day.

When it comes to new clothing, while the retail and advertising industries may see the Easter season as one more reason for a sales flyer, there is much more behind wearing something new than just looking good or starting Spring with the latest style.

Those who are newly baptized, whether at Easter or at another time during the year, receive a white garment to signify the new life they have taken on and the cleansing action of Baptism. The new or special clothes that the rest of the community wears at Easter honors the new life of these new Christians and reminds all of us of the gift we have been given in Baptism.

However, because we live in a culture that focuses *so* much on appearances, we can too easily miss the holistic connection between housecleaning or how we look and what is happening *inside* of us or our homes. A simple prayer of gratitude for our clothes—as we are dressing ourselves or helping our children get dressed—or for the home we seem to be endlessly trying to keep clean can help us to be a bit more mindful of the new life around us and within us.

After Baptism into *their* new life of faith at Easter, the newly initiated Christians, or neophytes, enter the last phase of their formation, that of **mystagogy** [MISS-ta-go-jee], or *mystagogia*, from the Greek meaning *to teach a doctrine or instruct into mysteries*. Originally, this meant gathering daily during the week after Easter to explore more fully the sacraments into which they had just been initiated. Today this involves several weeks of savoring what it means to be a Catholic Christian and of trying to understand more about what being a full part of the community means.

The idea of taking time to ponder a new experience like this can be helpful for all of us, especially mothers. When any change happens—with its own dying and rising—it can be very helpful to take some time to listen in faith to understand how God is a part of what is happening, to "reflect on it in our hearts," as Mary did. Pondering the ways that God is at work in our lives is an excellent habit— even for a brief moment, which may be all that a mom can grab—helping us to see things with new eyes.

MOTHERS' SPIRITUALITY
IS *COMPASSIONATE AND PATIENT*

As Jesus was dying on the cross, all the gospels record that Mary, his mother, and other women were among those nearby, looking on. And the gospels tell us that he had already been anointed by at least one woman in anticipation of his suffering and death.

Mothers often find themselves caring for and supporting those who are suffering, helping them in any way they can and being present to the other's pain, whether it's kissing an "owie" or helping someone grieve a death. Mothers' spirituality is compassionate because it *suffers with* another's pain, and it calls us to empathy as we watch those we love live with the effects of others' choices, as we have also done in our lives.

Mothers' spirituality isn't *passive*; mothers don't just let life happen to them. They meet it with a deep strength and help to bring about a lot of important change and growth, but they often do it in a different style, in a way that is often subtle and not as direct as a typical man's approach might be. They know, for example, that at times the most effective way to get something done may not always be the most direct, which can be very frustrating and puzzling to others in their lives. Even when mothers are in control in a situation, we generally tend to exercise that control in a rather indirect way, perhaps by hinting or telling a story to introduce a point or by requesting rather than requiring or demanding something from others.

This compassionate aspect of our spirituality includes the patient waiting that we explored during the season of Advent, in the hope we know that more may be happening than appears to be. As mothers deal with *the way things are*—often in situations that we have not helped create—at times we have a longer-range view, because we see how long growth can take—in ourselves, in our children, and in others around us—and at our best, we're willing to accept others as they are and to be with them in the pain they are experiencing now.

ACHIEVING A BALANCE

How can this compassionate and patient quality of mothers' spirituality be out of balance at times, as we try to listen to our own pain and that of others?

On the one hand, many times as mothers we can be *too concerned and too compassionate* in ways that do not allow others to work things out for themselves. It is not easy at all to allow others to cope with their pain and not rush in to "fix it." Except for very small children and infants, not only can we usually not "make it all better," but it's good for the other person that we *can't* at times. As much as we would rather not see the other in pain, it is usually not our responsibility, and our "help" would take away the growth and learning to which the other person is invited by this suffering.

As mothers, we can also be *too patient*, tolerating poor or unjust treatment from others at times. From the time we are young girls, women are still too often socialized to defer to others and to focus on what others may want or need, rather than ask for what they themselves need. The ability to be clear and to claim our own appropriate needs is not only important to us personally; it is also important in modeling healthy behavior for our children—our sons as well as our daughters.

When mothers *are* too patient or unclear about what they need or want in a situation, they may end up manipulating or being *too* indirect, using the guilt trips for which mothers are notorious, or even whining. Or, this frustration may show itself in playing the victim or blaming others rather than taking responsibility for our own lives. These patterns are warning signals that can alert us to take a look at the ways that we may be giving away our appropriate personal power without fully realizing it.

On the other hand, mothers may have *too little empathy and compassion* at times, perhaps because of an isolation or narrowness in their concerns, thinking, "I have enough to worry about already." It may even be due to the "compassion fatigue" that the information overload in our culture can spawn, especially about tragedy or injustice. At times we may also be too judgmental, unwilling to understand what a situation may be like from the other person's point of view, not "walking in the other's shoes for a while." Jesus cautions us in the gospels, "Do not judge, so that you may not be judged" (Matthew 7:1).

There are times, however, in the face of a situation that is clearly wrong, that it is important not to tolerate injustice, but it also may be helpful to examine the source of our frustration. Is there something we can *do* to change the situation? Are there other sources of information that we need to be able to more fully understand what is happening? Have we prayed for the grace to understand the situation and the wisdom to act well? And are we being patient enough and understanding *of ourselves*, so that we then have some energy available for understanding others?

Clarity about what we can change in our lives and what we can't is an important grace. The balance we are seeking here is the one reflected in the Serenity prayer, originally written by Dr. Reinhold Neibuhr in 1932 but made well known through Alcoholics Anonymous and other twelve-step groups:

> God, grant me the serenity to accept the things I cannot change, courage to change the things I can, and wisdom to know the difference, living one day at a time, enjoying one moment at a time, accepting hardship as the pathway to peace, taking, as [God] did, this sinful world as it is, not as I would have it, trusting that [God] will make all things right if I surrender to [God's] will, that I may be reasonably happy in this life and supremely happy with [God] forever in the next. Amen.

Knowing when to show compassion and patience in accepting the way things are and when to push for change *is* always a complicated judgment call. But it is essential in developing good balance as mothers to change what we can and also to be willing to suffer with others and with Jesus as we are called to live the paschal mystery in our lives.

MISCARRIAGE: AN EARLY LOSS

As we saw earlier, one way that the paschal mystery may unfold in a mother's life is in the experience of a miscarriage. As I started to talk to women friends about what had happened to me so unexpectedly, I began to realize that miscarriage is a fairly frequent occurrence, something that first-time moms aren't usually told about in order not to scare them.

A number of women told me that they had miscarried before their other children or that they had lost one or more pregnancies in between other live births. The rate of miscarriage is usually estimated at 10 to 20 percent. And 80 to 90 percent of the women who miscarry do so in their first pregnancy, although experts don't seem to know why. These women have a very high chance of bearing a healthy child the next time.

Later, I learned the reason for the miscarriage in my case. Because I have what is called an incompetent cervix, a condition with which I was born, I can't carry a pregnancy to term without a cervical purse-string stitch, a piece of cord which seals in the baby after a certain point in its development and which is removed a few weeks before labor is to begin, after which the birth can happen normally. If it weren't for this amazing technology in my later pregnancies, none of our three sons would be here.

With the experience of a miscarriage, there are many questions: Why did this happen? Is there something I/we should have done differently? And even: how can God allow this to happen? Because the mother has been far more directly connected to the pregnancy in the early stages, it may be harder for the father to "connect" to what has happened, especially since there's usually no body to grieve over. But they both have a right to grieve the loss of their child, a right it's often hard for others around the parents to understand.

Relatives and friends—if they even know that the miscarriage has happened—find it hard to know what to say to comfort those they care about at a time of loss. The usual comments—"You can always have another child," "Maybe it's just as well because it's nature's way of getting rid of imperfect children," or "It was God's will; now you have an angel in heaven. Maybe someday you'll understand it"—don't really acknowledge the deep pain that the parents are experiencing.

Parents who are trying to adopt often have a similar experience of loss when an adoption doesn't work out for any one of a number of reasons. Sometimes these are called adoptive miscarriages, but as a friend reminded me who had just gone through this wrenching situation, sometimes it's far more than a miscarriage. She and her husband had held the baby and spent days with her, by arrangement with her young birth mother, who then changed her mind under pressure from her family. And this can happen multiple times for adoptive parents.

Any kind of a miscarriage is hard on everyone concerned, and grieving it and beginning to heal from that loss or others like it is a complex process.

LOSS OF A PREGNANCY OR A CHILD: BEGINNING TO HEAL

The technical term for a miscarriage, a "spontaneous abortion," reminds us that, while there are some significant differences in the situations, women coping with the aftermath of an abortion often have similar experiences of loss to cope with: a pregnancy that ends without a baby and a child or children who died unborn. And these experiences also have some elements in common with those who are coping with the death of a child already born.

In the case of an abortion, in addition to the loss involved in a miscarriage, there is an additional dynamic of forgiveness needed in the healing from this experience. This includes forgiving those responsible for and involved in the abortion as well as forgiving oneself. The key questions that a woman who is struggling after an abortion has to resolve are: Can my child forgive me? Can God forgive me? Can I forgive myself?

When a child dies, whether it is a stillbirth or later on, it is an unspeakable tragedy. We know that this experience was even more common for mothers in the past before modern medical resources, but that doesn't make it any easier. With the death of a parent there is a loss of history, but with the death of a child the loss is of future hopes and dreams. It's a place where words fail us, and the only consolation is a wordless presence in faith and holding one another.

Whatever the source, these losses may trigger a variety of reactions in the women who have them, from depression to anger to sleep disorders to even drug and alcohol abuse. These are signs of the need for grieving to help heal the loss involved, and, unfortunately, our culture is notoriously poor at the task of mourning.

My grieving for the pregnancy we lost took a rather unusual form. Although I was supposed to stay in our apartment and rest after coming home from the hospital, I couldn't, so Mitch dropped me off at a park where I spent the day in prayer, telling God off. Just as I would get angry with a good friend if that's how I felt, it seemed appropriate to tell God how mad I was. There was plenty of crying and some yelling, too. (If anyone had walked by, I'm afraid they would have wondered about my sanity.)

After letting God have all my anger, I felt this tremendous peace and heard the words, "I want this child to be with Me now more than to be with you." (Let me quickly add that this is the only time that I have heard words while in prayer.) Our loss was still difficult to deal with, but the consolation that I experienced after being open about my feelings with God is hard to describe.

There are many ways to grieve and deal with a loss like this; Project Rachel and the National Office of Post-Abortion Reconciliation and Healing suggest some steps toward healing from the aftermath of an abortion, which also may apply in the case of a miscarriage and perhaps the death of a child. They emphasize that there is no fixed sequence and that some women may need help with this process, while others can do it alone.

Their suggestions include telling your story with all its pain and anger—probably more than once, grieving the loss—which may include both the loss of the child and at times the loss of the father for some women, naming the baby if there wasn't a name given, writing a letter to the child in which you can say all the things you need to say, and ritualizing your loss, using symbolic objects to help make the baby or child more concrete. (See the "Resources" section at the end of the book for how to contact Project Rachel.)

Those who have studied grieving remind us that the process of grief is exactly that: a *process*. Just as a woman who has had a child will always be a mom, so a woman who has lost a child will always be a bereaved mom. The pain will lessen with the years, but it will never completely leave, especially when faced with the simple questions people often ask, like, "Do you have any children? How many?" Sometimes, with the best intentions, a church community may ask mothers to stand on Mother's Day, a simple request which may bring up painful memories for women who have experienced such a loss.

Some local churches have made important efforts to help women and couples deal with the loss they've experienced. One parish began the process with the following bulletin announcement:

> We are planning to have a special Mass to honor the children of our parish who died before or very soon after they were born—particularly those who were not baptized and received neither a funeral nor a burial. Death may have been due to miscarriage, stillbirth, abortion, SIDS, etc. The lack of some kind of Catholic rite often leaves families with a sense of being ignored in their grief or that a life lost at such an early age is somehow less important to the Church and perhaps even less valuable to God. We at Saint Mary's wish to dispel that image. To do this tastefully and in a way that will most benefit the families who have suffered this type of loss, we are asking for input from those of you who have experienced such a death in your families. What would be most helpful for you? What, if anything, would you want to make sure did not occur at such a service? Your input may be anonymous. However, if you would like to come to a planning session, please join us on [date, place, time]. Our hope is that this Mass will serve in some way to be the funeral these tiny, never forgotten, and no-longer-ignored people of God never had.

As a result of this announcement and the planning that followed, this parish now has an annual Mass for the Unborn Dead to help mothers (and fathers) remember and heal from their losses.

Whether the loss is a miscarriage, an abortion, a still-birth, or a young child, the scripture passage from the prophet Jeremiah echoes through the centuries, "In Ramah is heard the sound of moaning, of bitter weeping! Rachel mourns her children, she refuses to be consoled because her children are no more" (31:15). In the prayer of tears many mothers can begin to sense a new depth of God's presence.

Some mothers are also finding that their experience in dealing with major losses, as well as the daily deaths and re-births in their lives as moms, helps them to be present and helpful to others who are facing death at the end of their lives, through organizations like Hospice. A couple of my friends involved with Hospice have remarked that, after be-ing present for a number of deaths, they were struck by how much dying can look a lot like birth—which is what our faith tells us, after all. Birth and death, dying and rising are, it seems, part of mothers' spirituality around the world.

MOTHERS AROUND THE WORLD: SPEAKING OUT

As much as tears and loss are a part of the lives of mothers in the more affluent and "developed" parts of our countries and our world, these concerns are then compounded in the poorer neighborhoods and countries of our world, places faced with violence, hunger, and repression that most of us can't begin to imagine. In a number of these situations, mothers have begun to find their collective political voice and power.

For example, the mothers of Latin America have been a powerful presence, especially in Argentina, Chile, and Guatemala, since the mid-1970s. The Madres (mothers) of the Plaza de Mayo, the main square in front of the Presi-dential Palace in Buenos Aires, have gathered every Thursday to remember those who have "disappeared,"—those who have been kidnapped without a trace or clue as to where they have been taken. Sara Ruddick, in her book *Maternal Thinking: Toward a Politics of Peace*, describes such a gathering:

> The Madres met each other outside hospitals or prisons, where they took food and other provisions and looked for traces of the disappeared, or outside government offices, where they tried, almost invariably without success, to get some accounting of their loved ones' whereabouts. When they marched the Madres wore white kerchiefs with the names of the disappeared embroidered on them. Often they carried lighted candles and almost always they wore or carried photographs of the disappeared. (p. 227)

They show impressive courage and worked together to handle their fears and to deal with necessary hazards, like tear gas. Although the women—both mothers and abuelas (grandmothers)—started their protests concerned for members of their own families, they have experienced a shift of concern. One woman from Chile put it this way: "Because of all this suffering we are united. I do not ask justice for my child alone, or the other women just for their children. We are asking for justice for all. All of us are equal. If we find one disappeared one I will rejoice as much as if they had found mine" (p. 231).

But what of mothers who aren't able to travel to poorer parts of the world or who are unable to be missionaries? How can they help with bigger issues that plague children and mothers here and elsewhere?

In a 2000 article in *U.S. Catholic* entitled "This Time It's Personal," Catholic columnist Dolores Curran told about her women's support group, whose members, now mostly retired, found themselves helping a Rwandan mother and her children.

Dolores' son had met this woman in his international humanitarian aid work, and she visited the women's group on a special visit to the United States.

> We sat on a member's patio on a glorious June morning while Nyoni captivated us with her story of life as a woman in Rwanda, her terrifying experiences during the genocide, and the fallout from the genocide that murdered nearly a million people. This fallout included a nation of trauma-tized children—75 percent of whom had witnessed at least one parent maimed or killed—widows with an average of eight children and no rights to land or welfare, and victims of rape as a weapon of war. (p. 34)

Nyoni shared her dream of coming to the United States to study so that she could help those victims in her own coun-try. After a series of adventures when a hoped-for scholarship for her didn't work out, Nyoni and her four children, whom she was rearing alone, ended up coming to this country only because the group of women and their various contacts were able to help raise more money than they ever thought possible, because it was for a *specific* purpose and person. Curran com-ments on how much the project helped the group itself:

> For years we wished aloud that we could improve the qual-ity of life for women and children in impoverished cultures, but the immense need always overwhelmed us. Where does one small group start?
>
> But when we were sent the opportunity to meet the needs of *one* woman with *one* child, our *one* small group rallied. For a year, our focus moved from ourselves to oth-ers, from personal problems to world problems, and from

caring to action. We learned that we possessed untapped resources, that it doesn't take a large organized group to achieve change, and that working together on a worthwhile project gave us a focus that brought us closer. (p. 35)

Mothers *are* a powerful force for change, one that has only begun to be tapped in a world that tolerates far too much violence and injustice. This process of mothers working to help accomplish change in conditions that endanger children is not limited to those in other countries.

Organizations like Mothers Against Drunk Driving (MADD) have helped make the roads safer for everyone, but they have their roots in mothers' action out of their own loss. MADD was founded by a small group of California women after a thirteen-year-old girl was killed by a hit-and-run drunk driver. He had been out of jail on bail for only two days for another hit-and-run drunk driving crash and had three previous drunk driving arrests and two convictions. The driver was allowed to plea bargain to manslaughter, and although he was sentenced to two years in prison, the judge allowed the offender to serve time in a work camp and, later, a halfway house. These mothers decided it was time to do something about a situation that affected *many* mothers' children through an organization which has been quite effective both in changing the sentencing of others charged with drunk driving and raising awareness about drinking and driving.

Whether it's the disappearance of family members or the danger posed by drunk drivers, when mothers band together, they can be an important force for hope and resurrection in the midst of a world that can seem to hold only death and despair.

EUCHARIST: SACRAMENT OF
THANKSGIVING AND COMMUNION

Dying and new life are at the heart of the sacrament that Jesus instituted at the Last Supper. In the face of his own death Jesus offered himself to his followers as food, as nourishment for them to live as he had, assuring them that he would always be with them when they shared a meal in memory of him.

And Christians have been amazingly faithful to that invitation throughout two millennia; in many languages throughout the world, through many rites and denominations, the Lord's Supper has been celebrated. Various Christian groups differ as to just how they understand the meaning of the Eucharist; for Catholics, Jesus is fully present in the bread and the wine, and they receive Jesus' body and blood when they receive communion.

British scholar Gregory Dix has pointed out that there are four movements described in the accounts that we have of the institution of the Eucharist and in other related scripture passages: in each case, they took the bread, said a blessing or gave thanks, broke the bread, and shared it. Let's examine each of these movements in light of mothers' experience.

First, *taking the bread and wine* implies a meal, since both were the staples of any meal in the Near Eastern culture. Meals and cooking are topics that mothers know well; they are usually the ones in charge of this literally life-giving aspect of family life. They know that food and the sharing of that food is often the shape that love takes.

Although family meals seem to be an endangered species in the too-fast culture in which we live, we know that eating together is an essential part of what makes us human—and what makes us a family. Besides the everyday meals, food and drink are also part of any special celebration, whether it's sharing birthday cake or holiday treats. At the Last Supper Jesus was probably celebrating the Passover meal with his apostles, a major Jewish feast. Food also brings us together at times of loss; taking a meal to someone who is sick or to a family after a death is a powerful way to try to comfort and to offer nourishment and comfort.

The second action described in each account was that of *saying a blessing or of giving thanks*, which is what the word "Eucharist" means: thanksgiving. Any meal really is already holy, whether a grace or blessing is said or not. When we gather to eat, we bring more than physical hunger to that situation; we bring a desire to share ourselves, to be nourished socially and completely. This is the perspective that has been lost in our convenience-based, on-the-run refueling approach to eating and food.

We recover this sense when we share a nice meal with friends or family—and plenty of time. Jesus was known for sharing meals and could be found at plenty of dinner parties, sharing food often with sinners and outcasts—a sign to his Jewish culture of the coming kingdom or reign of God.

When Jesus said, "This is my Body," he offered himself in a way that mothers are especially able to understand, as Joan Ohanneson suggests in her book *Woman: Survivor in the Church*:

> Women are able to enter into the Eucharist by laying additional claim to a flesh-and-blood consecration from their own life experience in childbearing. What is childbirth if not a literal offering up of one's body and blood for another? As the fruit of that offering, what is a newborn child but a kind of resurrection of the human race through rebirth? Indeed, what actually transpires during the nine-month gestation which occurs during pregnancy but a

gradual transformation of the mother's bread and wine (food and drink) into body and blood (Eucharist) in the form of another human being? (p. 32)

Whether they give birth or adopt, mothers continue to offer themselves and their lives for their children—and others—in many ways every day. This is part of the third action described, that of *breaking the bread*, a symbol of the dying and rising we have been exploring. During the liturgy of the Eucharist we describe the paschal mystery—the mystery of faith—several ways, including: "Dying you destroyed our death, rising you restored our life. Lord Jesus, come in glory."

In a very real sense, by witnessing this action and receiving the Eucharist, we are committing ourselves to be broken and poured out in love as Jesus was—sometimes in ways that we least expect.

Finally, *the bread and cup are given* to the disciples—and to us. St. Paul reminds us of the implications of this communion in his first letter to the Christians in Corinth: "Because the loaf of bread is one, we, though many, are one body, for we all partake of the one loaf" (10:17). Not only are we one with Jesus, we are *one with one another* and we *are* the body of Christ. This means that we are to share our food with everyone—especially the hungry—and this is deeply related to the communal quality of mothers' spirituality that we explored in the section on Advent.

And, after being nourished as the one body of Christ, we are sent forth to be Christ's presence in the world, in our own unique ways in our homes and families, and to be willing to be poured out and broken for others.

The liturgical reforms since the Second Vatican Council in the 1960s have encouraged a more full and conscious participation on the part of those gathered, calling us to be more than silent spectators at Mass and to be more aware of celebrating what we are living. In light of that focus, there is a very real sense in which as mothers *we* take the bread, bless it, break it and share it—with our children and our families and with our world.

The writer Andre Dubus, in making sandwiches for his daughters, glimpses what we as mothers are called to begin to see:

> . . . the sandwiches are sacraments. . . . If I could give my children my body to eat, again and again without losing it, my body like the loaves and fishes going endlessly into mouths and stomachs, I would do it. And each motion is a sacrament, this holding of plastic bags, of knives, of bread, of cutting board, this pushing of the chair, this spreading of mustard on bread, the trimming of liverwurst, of ham. All sacraments, as putting the lunches into a zippered book bag is. . . . even if I do not feel or acknowledge it, this is a sacrament. ("Epilogue" in Grady, pp. 223–224)

Hopefully, sharing the Eucharist helps us begin to see the sacraments all around us.

MOTHERS SPEAK

Mothers speak of their experience of the paschal mystery in their lives:

Everything seemed to be going perfectly for my second pregnancy—just like the first one. Then, at the beginning of my third month, my whole world came crashing down. I was hospitalized in the morning and by the afternoon I had miscarried.

Miscarriage—where did they come up with that word? I felt like it was a miscarriage all right—a miscarriage of justice. It wasn't fair. I wanted this baby. I loved her. She had been with me twenty-four hours a day for three months and now she was just gone. I went through a whole range of emotions from guilt to anger to overwhelming sadness. . . .

My husband did the best that he could—he tried to be strong and protect me, but that wasn't what I needed, either. I wanted this life to be acknowledged. I needed to talk. I wanted my questions answered. I needed to cry and to grieve this tremendous loss. I felt like no one else cared like I did. Mostly, I went through my grief alone.

When I was ready to work on further healing of the three miscarriages I had experienced, I needed a quiet place and some solitude. So I went to the chapel, sat down on the floor and mentally and spiritually placed myself in the presence of Christ, at the foot of his cross. I was familiar with the use of present-time guided imagery in prayer, and felt called to use it as a healing tool.

I began by reading the story of Jesus and the children that Fr. Bob had just shared with us. I reminded myself of how much Jesus loves all children. I particularly thought of how much Jesus loves my little ones—much more and much better than I ever could.

Then, one by one, I asked Jesus to bring my miscarried children to me. I didn't really know what to expect, but I felt God's invitation to empty myself and trust. . . .

[After the other two] I saw Jesus bring Zachary, the youngest, to me. He was a bright, happy little four-year-old (the age he would have been if he had lived.) Tugging at Jesus to hurry, he seemed very eager to come to me. He ran up and threw his arms around my neck. He chattered about how happy he was to be with me and how much fun he was having with everyone where he lived. It made me think of times when I had picked one of my other children up from a party when they were small and how they would chatter on in great detail about all the fun they'd had.

It was impossible for me to feel anything but Zachary's joy as he continued to tell me how much he would like it when I came to live where he did. I spent some time just enjoying being with him.

Then he was ready to return to his home. As I kissed him goodbye and began to take him to Jesus, he let go of my hand and eagerly rushed on ahead. (Just like any four year old would!) I had no sense of being abandoned. What I did feel was an overwhelming sense of gratitude that my little child was so happy.

It took a time of tears and silence before I could begin to gather myself together. When I did, my prayer was one of thanksgiving to God who is the perfect father and the perfect mother to my children.

I finally felt free from the selfishness that had been very much a part of my pain. I no longer felt any desire to have been able to keep these children from their ideal, eternal home. I was, and I continue to be, grateful for the happiness and freedom they now have. I sensed an eternal link with them that was and is the love we have shared since their conception.

The most powerful experience I've had as a mother is a recurring one—the realization of how absolutely deep and powerful love becomes when you give birth to a baby, how that love intensifies when you see them hurting or struggling, and how that love almost crushes you when you lose one by death.

I have lost two sons, one by suicide, one by murder, and it was the love they brought into my life that made it possible for me to survive these tragic losses. This love never left me. Remembering their lives, with so much love, kept my sons close to me as the years went by. Almost like a revelation, it was this love that broke the time barrier that had separated us, and I learned that I live now in both worlds, mine and theirs. Love keeps us joined and is the promise that my future, like their present, is eternity.

The most painful experience I had as a mother was when our eighteen-year-old son had to testify against a peer regarding a very serious crime that would send his former fellow soccer player and high school peer to adult prison for a very long time. This was a wake-up call to our son in a most profound sense—it put him in danger in the short term and will also possibly endanger him once this individual is released from prison.

I have had to take this to Mary, the Mother of Jesus, as she experienced not only a son that stood for right and truth at the threat of danger to her son, but the threat became a most dangerous reality. Mary witnessed the torture and death of her only son, who had done nothing wrong to deserve such a fate. Mary can console my fears and grant me comfort.

I remember a day in June, not too many years ago, when I came home from work and found mail announcing some kind of honor for at least two of my sons, and at that time, they were all doing well and celebrating one thing or another. I remember feeling so proud and happy and thanked God for the moment, because at the same time I was aware that all of that is fleeting—I knew that other times would follow that would not be so smooth or feel so rewarding. I took that joy of the moment and "treasured it in my heart" and pull it up on a regular basis. It gives me hope.

I also try to take the hard things and "treasure them in my heart," and here "treasure" feels more like keeping them in my heart in a way that allows me to walk with my kids through their trials—when they share them with me. Not that I can fix them, or should even try to, but I can try to be present with them, holding their hands, their hearts in mine, and commending them to God's tender love, which is so much more than mine. This seems to involve few words; it's more like a presence. But all these things I treasure in my heart. I find that I don't do it well when I am living in fear of whatever or when I am not living, for the most part, in the present moment.

MODELS FROM THE TRADITION

When we look to the saints and others for models of new life and the paschal mystery in mothers' spirituality, three examples that come to mind are Rose Hawthorne Lathrop, Dorothy Day, and Sr. Helen Prejean.

Rose Hawthorne Lathrop (1851–1926) was the third and favorite child of the famous American author Nathaniel Hawthorne, but both of her parents died while she was in her teens, and by the age of twenty she was married to George Lathrop, a promising young man. Unfortunately, the death of their only son at an early age and George's drinking problems contributed to the deterioration of their marriage and their eventual separation. She and George had both become Catholic, and gradually Rose found herself drawn to the care of those with incurable cancer, patients who were not allowed at that time to stay in hospitals after a terminal diagnosis.

Rose was especially concerned about the poor who had no one to tend to them, those for whom she felt called to provide friendship, dignity, and respect. She gradually devoted her life to caring for those dying of cancer, and others joined her in what became the Dominican order of the Servants of Relief for Incurable Cancer, a religious community which is still active in this ministry in a number of homes around the country. They continue to follow a strict rule set by their founder: no money is accepted from patients, their families, or the state.

Like Rose Hawthorne, many women—mothers, nurses, friends, and those in religious communities—continue to care faithfully day in and day out for those who are sick and dying, both in their families and in many other settings, and to give them a hope and dignity that they would not otherwise have.

Rose's example of trusting in God's providence helped inspire **Dorothy Day** (1897–1980), a young woman who was reading a biography of Ms. Hawthorne Lathrop when she decided to launch the newspaper *The Catholic Worker*. With Peter Maurin, an itinerant philosopher and radical, she founded the Catholic Worker Movement, which resulted in soup kitchens and houses of hospitality for the poor and a political movement to help change the system so that such charity would not be needed.

It was the birth of Dorothy's daughter that precipitated her conversion to Catholicism and the painful end to her common-law marriage and many of her socialist connections. She brought a deep love of the poor from her radical background with her into the Church and helped remind us all to see Jesus in the poor, that what we do for them we do to Him.

In speaking about Dorothy as a model of the connection between liturgy and justice, Fr. Theodore Ross, SJ, explains:

> Day could not go to Communion and be insensitive to the reality that someone was hungry; she could not enjoy the warmth of Eucharistic consolation and know that she had a blanket while her brother or sister did not; she could not "go the altar of God" and be aware that someone was sleeping over a grate on the sidewalk. (in Hughes and Francis, p. 27)

Dorothy was clearly a woman of the twentieth century, ahead of her time in many ways and said by some to be the most influential figure in American Catholicism. Not only did she practice works of charity, she was also committed to work for social change and justice, to help new possibilities emerge from the radical perspective of the Gospels. Her work lives on in the many Catholic Worker communities today across the country, and the *Catholic Worker* paper still sells for a penny a copy.

Dorothy Day's practical charity is also a part of many mothers' lives; whenever mothers continue to feed the hungry—in their own families as well as outside it—and work to change social structures, they honor her thirst for justice.

Sister Helen Prejean, the most contemporary of these women, also shows us a thirst for justice as she deals with the paschal mystery today. Born in 1939 in Baton Rouge, Louisiana, she joined the Sisters of St. Joseph of Medaille in 1957. She has worked in various positions in ministry for her community, and while living in the St. Thomas housing project after having dedicated her life to the poor of New Orleans, she became pen pals with Patrick Sonnier, the convicted killer of two teenagers, sentenced to die in the electric chair of Louisiana's Angola State Prison.

Upon Sonnier's request, Sister Helen repeatedly visited him as his spiritual advisor. In doing so, her eyes were opened to the Louisiana execution process. She began her prison ministry and turned her experiences into the book *Dead Man Walking: An Eyewitness Account of the Death Penalty in the United States*, which has been an international bestseller and was made into a major motion picture.

Fifteen years after beginning her crusade, Sister Helen has witnessed five executions in Louisiana and today educates the public about the death penalty by lecturing, organizing, and writing. As the founder of Survive, a victim's advocacy group in New Orleans, she continues to counsel not only inmates on death row, but the families of murder victims as well.

Whether it's facing death row, the death or disappearance of a family member, or even the death of hopes and dreams, women and mothers like Sister Helen Prejean have been there—to face death and to accompany others as they do so.

SCRIPTURE FOR REFLECTION

As we reflect on our own lives as mothers the dying and rising of the paschal mystery, the following passages may be helpful. Please try to take some time with one or more of these passages and with the questions following them. You may prefer to reflect on these with other mothers.

[Jesus] got up from the table, took off his outer robe, and tied a towel around himself. Then he poured water into a basin and began to wash the disciples' feet and to wipe them with the towel that was tied around him. . . . After he had washed their feet, had put on his robe, and had returned to the table, he said to them, "Do you know what I have done to you? You call me Teacher and Lord—and you are right, for that is what I am. So if I, your Lord and Teacher, have washed your feet, you also ought to wash one another's feet. For I have set you an example, that you also should do as I have done to you. (John 13:4–5, 12–15)

—*Try to picture this scene and feel what it would feel like to have Jesus wash and dry your feet.*
—*Whose feet have you washed lately—that is, whom have you served lately? How? Has anyone "washed your feet"? Who?*
—*Which was more challenging for you: to serve or be served? Why?*

Standing near the cross of Jesus were his mother, and his mother's sister, Mary the wife of Clopas, and Mary Magdalene. When Jesus saw his mother and the disciple whom he loved standing beside her, he said to his mother, "Woman, here is your son." Then he said to the disciple, "Here is your mother." And from that hour the disciple took her into his own home. (John 19:25–27)

—*Imagine how Mary must have felt as she stood beneath the cross. What would it have been like to be there with her?*
—*Who else has been "mother" to you besides your own? Is Mary a mother for you? Why or why not?*
—*Whom have you accompanied in a time of grief? Was that difficult for you?*

Mary [Magdalene] stood weeping outside the tomb. As she wept, she bent over to look into the tomb; and she saw two angels in white, sitting where the body of Jesus had been lying, one at the head and the other at the feet. They said to her, "Woman, why are you weeping?" She said to them, "They have taken away my Lord, and I do not know where they have laid him." When she had said this, she turned around and saw Jesus standing there, but she did not know that it was Jesus. Jesus said to her, "Woman, why are you weeping? Whom are you looking for?" Supposing him to be the gardener, she said to him, "Sir, if you have carried him away, tell me where you have laid him, and I will take him away." Jesus said to her, "Mary!" She turned and said to him in Hebrew, "Rabbouni!" [which means teacher]. Jesus said to her, "Do not hold on to me, because I have not yet ascended to the Father. But go to my brothers and say to them, 'I am ascending to my Father and your Father, to my God and your God.'" Mary Magdalene went and announced to the disciples, "I have seen the Lord"; and she told them that he had said these things to her. (John 20:11–18)

—*Recall a time of grief or deep loss. Did you feel God's presence? If so, how?*

—*Put yourself in Mary Magdalene's position and listen to Jesus call your name tenderly. How does that feel?*

Other Scripture Passages to Explore

John 12:24–26—Unless a grain of wheat dies, it cannot live more fully.

Luke 7:11–15—Jesus brings back to life the only son of the widow of Nain.

Questions for Individual or Group Reflection

If you had to name the stations of the cross in your life, what would those be?

When you prepare a meal, do you experience that as holy? If so, how and when?

An especially memorable meal that I can recall was . . .

What has "nourished" or "fed" you lately? How are you "nourishing" or "feeding" your spirit?

Describe a recent personal experience of the paschal mystery, where the death of what had been led to new possibilities that you couldn't have imagined?

A powerful symbol of new life for me is . . .

Resources for This Season
The following are some resources related to the themes explored here; full information on these can be found at the end of this book.

Jaworski, *Praying the Stations with the Women of the World*
MADD
Project Rachel
Rupp, *Your Sorrow Is My Sorrow*
Schut, *Food and Faith*
Tickle and Lafser, *An Empty Cradle, a Full Heart*

Chapter Five

PENTECOST
The Spirit at Work

Judith was delighted with the present she had thought of for her daughter's high school graduation next spring. She would ask a number of women friends to write about what their lives were like when *they* were eighteen and what they have learned since then. She would then collect these reflections and give them to her daughter. Judith was convinced that the wisdom those women could share with Ann was worth more than any other present she could buy for her daughter.

Judith has a strong respect for the wisdom of women and mothers, and wisdom is one of the many gifts given by the Holy Spirit, whose coming we celebrate on Pentecost.

WHAT IS THIS SEASON?

The feast of Pentecost (from the Greek for "fiftieth") comes on the fiftieth day after Easter, ending the Easter season. Before Christian times this was a Jewish harvest festival of thanksgiving for the first fruits and for the covenant; it was also called the Feast of Weeks, seven weeks plus one after the great feast of Passover. Besides the term "Pentecost," Christians sometimes refer to this feast as "Whitsunday," which refers to the white garments that the neophytes, the newly baptized, originally wore for the fifty days of the Easter season, until this day.

Pentecost is also sometimes called the "birthday of the Church," because the Acts of the Apostles record an amazing transformation: the followers of Jesus shivering behind locked doors in an upper room become people "on fire" with love of God, preaching so enthusiastically that some who saw them figured they must be drunk.

The change? An experience of the Spirit of God so powerful that the book of Acts uses vivid images of wind and flames to try to describe this invisible but very real energy—an electricity of sorts—at work in them. And that amazing energy gave them the ability to communicate and to understand each other in a way that impressed everyone. We read:

> And they were all filled with the holy Spirit and began to speak in different tongues, as the Spirit enabled them to proclaim. Now there were devout Jews from every nation under heaven staying in Jerusalem. At this sound, they gathered in a large crowd, but they were confused because each one heard them speaking in his own language. They were astounded, and in amazement they asked, "Are not all these people who are speaking Galileans? Then how does each of us hear them in his own native language?" (Acts 2:4–8)

This experience of understanding each other across many differences is in direct contrast to the story of the Tower of Babel found in the book of Genesis, chapter 11. That account depicts the beginning of diverse languages and the confusion that has resulted ever since because of the people planning to build a tower to heaven, trying to reach up to God—on human terms. This Babel story can sound all too familiar today, as our society attempts to reach higher and further in all kinds of ways—and in the process creates ever more noise pollution around us.

Instead of that cacophony, the first apostles and disciples found that the Spirit's power allowed them to not only listen to *their own* hearts and longings but also to understand others around them. When we are divided among ourselves and within ourselves at times, we long for the inspiration and the energy that they experienced through the Holy Spirit.

For the earliest Christians the feast of Pentecost also was the time to celebrate Jesus' ascension into heaven, but by the fourth century these two feasts were becoming separate. Since then, the ascension has been celebrated on the fortieth day after Easter, Ascension Thursday, but in some places it is now observed on the following Sunday.

The feast of the Ascension commemorates Jesus finally leaving his disciples behind to carry on his message, after he first appears to them a number of times after his death to reassure them and teach them further. It was only when Jesus had left his followers that the power of the Spirit could help them understand the full implications of who Jesus was and of the message they had been chosen to share with the world.

Likewise, mothers often see the evidence of their teaching and influence on their children only *after* those offspring have left home and become independent; Mom suddenly seems to have learned far more than she ever knew when they were still living at home. And these mothers especially pray for the Holy Spirit's presence with their young adult children, as they are now making decisions with weightier consequences.

FROM THE TRADITION

What practices from the Christian tradition can help enhance our appreciation of the coming of the Holy Spirit, which we celebrate at Pentecost?

The days between the feasts of the Ascension and of Pentecost were traditionally a time of prayer in the Church, in union with the apostles as they prayed for the gift of the Spirit. This was the origin of the devotion known as the **novena**, from the Latin word for "nine," a time of nine days of prayer. Sometimes these nine days are consecutive—perhaps before a special liturgical feast or a personal event or need, such as a wedding or surgery—or at times they may be the same day of the week, such as nine First Fridays or nine Mondays. A novena can be either a private or a communal devotion; either way, prayer for others and for ourselves is always helpful and powerful, as we will explore further in the section on ordinary time.

Christian prayer is addressed to the **Trinity**, the three persons in one God, usually expressed as Father, Son, and Holy Spirit. This is a key teaching for Christians: that we are saved by God the Father through Jesus Christ in the power of the Holy Spirit. Although at the end of Matthew's gospel Jesus commands that Christians baptize in the name of the Father, Son, and Spirit, it was not until the fourth and fifth centuries that this teaching was clarified, against those who taught that Jesus was not fully equal to God. This doctrine continued to be further refined through the Middle Ages and is a mystery that has remained at the heart of Christian thought about who God is.

How do mothers today begin to make sense of one God as three persons, an idea which can seem quite abstract? Theologian Elizabeth Johnson has suggested that the

Trinity tells us much about the importance of relationship, friendship, and mutuality. In *She Who Is: The Mystery of God in Feminist Theological Discourse*, she explains:

> The God who is thrice personal signifies that the very essence of God is to be in relation, and thus relatedness rather than the solitary ego is the heart of all reality. . . . [And] at the heart of holy mystery is not monarchy but community; not an absolute ruler but a threefold *koinonia* [that is, community]. (pp. 215–216)

Thinking about God as relationship and friendship was often avoided in classical theology because of a concern that stressing the mutuality of the divine persons might blur their distinctness, but mothers know that friendship *doesn't* blur personalities but rather helps them to be more vivid and distinct. We also know that friendship at its best can be a little glimpse of God and God's love.

In the midst our hierarchical world, the radical oneness and mutuality at the heart of God is often hard to imagine or envision; one image that has been suggested is that of a round dance, with no real beginning or end. Whether we find the model of three friends in an unending dance or St. Patrick's famous shamrock or some other image useful, the *unity in the diversity* within God challenges both our minds and our imaginations.

One way that we have of recalling the Trinity in our daily life and prayer is the **Sign of the Cross**, which begins and ends the liturgy of the Eucharist and much of our Christian prayer. We know this custom existed early in the church because the writer Tertullian already refers to it in the third century. At first the cross was drawn on the forehead with the right thumb; later in the Western church it was made by using the right hand to go from forehead to breast and from left shoulder to right shoulder. The idea, whether in private prayer or in public liturgical celebration, was to remember that our whole selves are loved by God as the Trinity.

Besides using the sign of the cross in their own prayer, moms often use the older form of tracing the cross on the forehead when they give a blessing to their children, whether tucking them in each night or at another time in the day, such as leaving for school or for a trip. When a mother blesses her child, she knows that she is asking God to be with this child in a special way.

The Holy Spirit, the third person of the Trinity, is associated with particular qualities or gifts. The seven **gifts of the Holy Spirit** in Catholic theology, a list that comes largely from the eleventh chapter of the book of the prophet Isaiah, are: wisdom, understanding, counsel, fortitude, knowledge, piety, and fear of the Lord. These are gifts that help us to live out the faith that is itself a gift of the Spirit; they aren't given to us to keep to ourselves but they are rather to be shared with others to help build up the community of faith.

So, for example, when Ann's daughter comes to her and asks her what to do about a friend who has been verbally demeaning some of their mutual friends and Ann says just the right thing after breathing a quick prayer for help, it's the gift of counsel from the Holy Spirit. And when Robin was able to hold things together after her husband's death with three little ones to take care of, she showed the gift of fortitude—she knew that God would not give her more than she could handle and, thus, did not turn bitter at what she faced alone. When we ask for what we need, the Spirit is indeed generous in answering us with gifts that we may not know are there until the situation calls them forth. And sometimes others can see these gifts in us far more easily than we can see them in ourselves.

MOTHERS' SPIRITUALITY IS
WONDERING AND *IMAGINATIVE*

The last of the seven gifts of the Holy Spirit usually mentioned is that of fear of the Lord. Theologians tell us that it refers more to the attitude of respect and awe that we are to have toward God—who is so much more than we can ever comprehend—rather than the usual idea of "fear." This wonder and reverence toward God is a quality that we mothers approach in a rather unique way because of our experience with children.

In the midst of the multitude of questions that children pose about the world around them and of the many ways that they can challenge the way we live, they invite us to fresh categories of meaning. As a result, they nudge our spirituality to be more aware, more open to wonder and delight, more inventive, resourceful, spontaneous, and even interruptible.

When we spend time as mothers with little ones and not-so-little ones who are exploring the world around them and who are themselves such amazing and ever-changing mysteries, we have a "front row seat" for a sense of wonder both at them and at the world that we are rediscovering through their eyes. Whether it's an infant discovering her toes, a toddler blowing bubbles, an adolescent in love, or a child delighting in bugs on the sidewalk or the first snow of the year, our children have much to teach us about how incredibly fascinating the world around us is.

Their discoveries of everything in life help us begin to realize that there are *far more* than seven "small-s" sacraments, that if we look far enough into anything "material" we will see the Spirit at work there, and that, as poets like Elizabeth Barrett Browning remind us, "Earth's crammed with heaven, And every common bush afire with God."

Because it's their job to explore the universe around them, our children help us to become more aware of process and experimentation, but at least for awhile our lives don't stand much chance of being very scheduled and structured. Tillie Olsen explains what happens to our organization:

> More than in any other human relationship, overwhelmingly more, motherhood means being instantly interruptable, responsive, responsible. Children need one *now* (and remember, in our society, the family must often try to be the center for love and health the outside world is not). The very fact that these are real needs, that one feels them as one's own (love, not duty), *that there is no one else responsible for these needs,* gives them primacy. It is distraction, not meditation, that becomes habitual; interruption, not continuity; spasmodic, not constant toil. (Cunneen, p. 81)

Although it's certainly messy and frustrating at times, this wonder-filled, flexible, playful spirituality can be a place of grace for us, calling us to *re-spect*—literally, to look again at—all that is around us.

ACHIEVING A BALANCE

How can this imaginative and wondering quality to our spirituality, this ability to entertain new possibilities and play with the imagination as we watch our children discover the world anew, get out of balance at times?

On the one hand, we can easily find ourselves *"too busy" to take time* for what our children have to teach us about the miracles around us. I think that this was what my dad was cautioning me about when he would stop by to visit in the years when I was home with three little ones under the age of four. One day as he was leaving and I had two little ones hanging on my legs and the baby in my arms, he told me, "Just remember, Kathy: these are the good old days."

At the time I thought ruefully, "Oh, sure, it's easy for you to say that as you're headed off to be with *adults* and to have real conversations and not to have to wipe noses or bottoms or clean up spilled food every few minutes!" But the more I thought about his words, the more I realized that he was telling me, "I wish *I* had realized when you and your siblings were growing up how important these times are. Don't let these days go by too fast; they are so important." There *are* things to be done and a house to be kept up, but there are also little ones to be delighted in, special people who sometimes can't wait to invite us to deeper sense of wonder and awe. This is a big part of what the tradition of sabbath invites us to: taking time to enjoy all of creation.

On the other hand, as much as we need to be open to what our children can teach us about looking at the world with new eyes, we also need to *be the adult presence* and source of safety that they need, to give them some structure and appropriate boundaries, a safe and fairly clean environment in which their wonder and delight can take shape.

But generally, as mothers we tend to do the *adult* part fairly well; the challenge for us is to "become like little children" a bit more, as Jesus encouraged us, and let them teach us.

THE HOLY SPIRIT: HOLY ENERGY

As we try to balance our sense of wonder as mothers, we also wonder: who *is* this Holy Spirit, so prominent in the season of Pentecost, and how can we speak of the power of this

Spirit? Although we must use metaphors to talk about God because God is always so much more than anything we can understand, the need for metaphors seems especially strong when it comes to speaking of the Holy Spirit; before long we find ourselves using images and poetry.

In general, when we talk about the Spirit, we are describing God's action and power in the world. In scripture we find the images of water and light, of fire and wind used for the Spirit—all of them elements without specific shape but with a definite impact on the world around them. However, these metaphors are not *personal*, like referring to God as Father and Son; in her book *Models of God: Theology for an Ecological, Nuclear Age*, Sally McFague suggests another possibility: seeing the Trinitarian God as Mother, Lover, and Friend, because the image of friendship for the Holy Spirit helps us to better appreciate God's personal relationship with the world. (We'll return to the notion of God as Mother a little later.)

However we image the Spirit, what does this Spirit *do* in our world? In a word, plenty. Elizabeth Johnson, in *She Who Is*, beautifully describes the action of what she calls Spirit-Sophia:

> She initiates novelty, instigates change, transforms what is dead into new stretches of life. Fertility is intimately related to her recreative power, as is the attractiveness of sex. It is she who is ultimately playful, fascinating, pure and wise, luring human beings into the depths of love. As mover and encourager of what tends toward stasis, Spirit-Sophia inspires human creativity and joy in the struggle. Wherever the gift of healing and liberation in however partial a manner reaches the winterized or damaged earth, or peoples crushed by war and injustice, or individual persons weary, harmed, sick, or lost on life's journey, there the new creation in the Spirit is happening. (p. 135)

As we look more closely, we find the Spirit all around us—dancing, whispering, delighting, encouraging, and especially giving life, bringing justice and liberation, and helping build up the community of believers. We find the Spirit *giving life* from the very beginning of scripture—as the wind hovering over the waters in creation—to the last book of the New Testament, the book of Revelation—in fact, saying there, "I am the Alpha and the Omega, the first and the last, the beginning and the end" (Revelation 22:13). The Spirit is creative and life giving, not just *initiating* life but *in every part of the process*, wherever new possibilities are emerging. When Patricia watches her husband willing to struggle with his alcoholism, for example, she believes that it is the Holy Spirit giving him the energy and the life to continue in his recovery.

The Spirit also brings about *justice and liberation*. The prophet Isaiah describes it well: "The spirit of the Lord GOD is upon me, because the LORD has anointed me; he has sent me to bring good news to the oppressed, to bind up the brokenhearted, to proclaim liberty to the captives, and release to the prisoners" (61:1).

And in Luke's gospel Jesus chooses to read this very passage when he goes to his hometown synagogue to announce the coming of the Reign of God. We read: "And he rolled up the scroll, gave it back to the attendant, and sat down. The eyes of all in the synagogue were fixed on him. Then he began to say to them, 'Today this scripture has been fulfilled in your hearing'" (Luke 4:20–21). Jesus knew that his power was from the Spirit, a power he had already received at his baptism by John the Baptist in the Jordan River.

Women like Betty Williams and Mairead Corrigan—one a mother and one an aunt, one a Catholic and one a

Protestant—show us the Spirit working through those who are trying to help build a more just world. Both women could no longer tolerate the violence around them in Northern Ireland, as they watched those they loved being killed. Together they helped create an organization for peace and were later awarded the Nobel Peace Prize in 1976.

Another function of the Spirit is to *build up the community of faith*. Jesus tells his disciples that the Spirit will come to them after he leaves, to help them and to keep them close to one another and close to God. One way we see the Spirit at work today is in gradually drawing the Christian churches into greater unity with each other in the ecumenical movement as they work on common projects and share facilities and resources.

It's important for us to remember, however, that the presence of the Spirit in our midst doesn't mean an absence of problems, divisions, and pettiness—for the first Christians or for us. There were already difficulties with each other in the earliest communities, and we also hear St. Paul reminding his followers that the Spirit calls them to be one. The Spirit *will* be there to inspire and help lead, but that presence will happen in the midst of our all-too-human faults—then and now.

Most Christians, essayist Annie Dillard complains in *Teaching a Stone to Talk*, are oblivious to the power of the Spirit in their midst. She observes, as only a poet can:

Does anyone have the foggiest idea what sort of power we so blithely invoke? Or, as I suspect, does no one believe a word of it? The churches are children playing on the floor with their chemistry sets, mixing up a batch of TNT to kill a Sunday morning. It is madness to wear ladies' straw hats and velvet hats to church; we should all be wearing crash helmets. Ushers should issue life preservers and signal flares; they should lash us to our pews. (p. 40)

In the twentieth century we have seen an especially powerful example of this "dangerous" Holy Spirit at work in the Second Vatican Council, held between October 1962 and December 1965.

Elected as an old man, Pope John XXIII stunned the world and the Catholic church when he called for the council, one that would not condemn heresy or threats to the faith, as in the past; rather, its goal was to help the church come to terms with the contemporary world through a process of *aggiornamento*, Italian for "bringing up to date." Pope John called for a new Pentecost in the Church and a process of "reading the signs of the times," of opening the windows to bring in the fresh air of the Spirit.

This was a larger and more ecumenical gathering than Rome had ever seen for a church council—with over 3,000 participants from all parts of the world, including bishops of all nationalities, invited observers from most Christian denominations, and even a few women. From the beginning it became clear that the bishops who gathered would not just approve the documents carefully prepared by the Vatican bureaucracy; rather, they debated and finally approved important documents that have re-energized the Catholic church and the Christian community in its dialogue with the contemporary world ever since.

The power of the Spirit is at work in many ways in our midst, stirring us up and calling us to help make our relationships with one another more life giving, more just, and more open to one another. When, as mothers, we see these qualities emerging in our families, our communities, and our world, we are know the energy of the Spirit is at work.

SOPHIA: THE WISDOM OF GOD

Besides wisdom being a gift of the Holy Spirit, it also has a special place in scripture, especially in the Old Testament. In many parts of the ancient Near East there was a strong tradition of reverence for, and literature about, wisdom—both the practical sort and the more philosophical kind. In scripture, when wisdom is described as a quality, wisdom is an "it." But when wisdom is referred to as a person—as it often is in the books of Proverbs, Wisdom, and Sirach, as well as some other places—Wisdom is referred to as a "she," Lady Wisdom; in Greek holy wisdom is *Hagia Sophia*.

Wisdom is spoken of as being there at the creation of the world, setting a banquet for those who will listen to her, bringing peace and security to those who obey her, and telling us that the way to her is through the fear of the Lord, the respect and awe for God that we discussed earlier. This clearly feminine Wisdom seems to be a communication of God through creation to humanity. Some have connected the figure of Wisdom with the Holy Spirit; others with Jesus as the Word.

Although the early church seems to have known Sophia well, there were concerns about devotion to Wisdom getting confused with the goddess worship that was still common then. Also, the early Christians tried to distance themselves from the Gnostics, a group that had a special devotion to Sophia but who also rejected the importance of the material world. For these and other reasons, the devotion to Wisdom was lost for many centuries but is now beginning to be rediscovered.

Mothers know a deep wisdom within themselves, deeper than words. They see it in their mothers and grandmothers and in other women of strength and insight—an important but elusive quality. It is deeply feminine, earthy, patient, open to all of life, deeply contemplative and, yet, quite practical—very difficult to describe but something we know when we see and hear it. As we mothers teach our children about life, we know that, if we listen, we will often learn just what it is that *we* also needed to learn.

Wisdom gets handed on from one mother to another in various ways, usually without any specific forms or traditions. But as women come to honor their own wisdom more, they find that they can also honor the aging process, which is so often linked with wisdom. In contrast to our youth-obsessed culture, they can see that the season of menopause and beyond offers them a rich time in their lives and a different energy that they can share with other women and mothers. The power of this wisdom of mothers also makes it easy for most mothers to imagine God as a mother.

GOD AS MOTHER: NURTURING LOVE

Pope John Paul I, who lived only thirty-three days after being elected as Pope in August 1978, left us with much to think about for such a short public presence. One of his most famous comments was, "God is a Father, but even more a Mother." He was indeed "on to" something, as we would say. Despite the fact that the Christian tradition has mainly used the masculine pronoun to refer to God, there are a surprising number of images of God as a mother or like a mother, both in scripture and other Christian sources.

Although Genesis does not image God as Creator this way, elsewhere in the Old Testament God is at times spoken of as giving birth to all of creation. For example, in Deuteronomy Moses is reminding the people of Israel of their covenant, their relationship with God before he dies, and in his song he tells them: "You were unmindful of the Rock that bore you; you forgot the God who gave you birth" (Deuteronomy 32:18).

When Job has questioned God about all his misfortunes and why evil happens, God's response uses first the masculine images of a builder and then a very feminine image, complete with "diapering" with swaddling bands and "babyproofing":

> Where were you when I laid the foundation of the earth? Tell me, if you have understanding. Who determined its measurements—surely you know! Or who stretched the line upon it? On what were its bases sunk, or who laid its cornerstone when the morning stars sang together and all the heavenly beings shouted for joy? Or who shut in the sea with doors when it burst out from the womb?—When I made the clouds its garment, and thick darkness its swaddling band, and prescribed bounds for it, and set bars and doors, and said, "Thus far shall you come, and no farther, and here shall your proud waves be stopped"? (Job 38:4–11)

In Isaiah we see first the masculine image of soldier used to talk about God's reaction to Israel's disobedience and then the image of a mother writhing in labor pains:

> The LORD goes forth like a soldier, like a warrior he stirs up his fury; he cries out, he shouts aloud, he shows himself mighty against his foes. For a long time I have held my peace, I have kept still and restrained myself; now I will cry out like a woman in labor, I will gasp and pant. (Isaiah 42:13–14)

There are other references that mention God nursing us at the breast. Moses, for example, is arguing with God and telling God that taking care of "the kids" is God's job, the traditional job of the mother:

> So Moses said to the LORD, "Why have you treated your servant so badly? Why have I not found favor in your sight, that you lay the burden of all this people on me? Did I conceive all this people? Did I give birth to them, that you should say to me, 'Carry them in your bosom, as a nurse carries a sucking child,' to the land that you promised on oath to their ancestors? . . . I am not able to carry all this people alone, for they are too heavy for me. (Numbers 11:11–12, 14)

In the prophet Hosea, God is described as a tender parent, whose actions are typically those of a mother, especially in the Hebrew culture:

> When Israel was a child, I loved him, and out of Egypt I called my son. The more I called them, the more they went from me. . . . Yet it was I who taught Ephraim to walk, I took them up in my arms; but they did not know that I healed them. I led them with cords of human kindness, with bands of love. I was to them like those who lift infants to their cheeks. I bent down to them and fed them. (Hosea 11:1–4)

Even Psalm 22, a cry for help to God in time of trial that Jesus may have prayed from the cross, talks about God as midwife, one who is perhaps helping in the "birth pangs" of a new creation as Jesus dies:

> Yet it was you who took me from the womb; you kept me safe on my mother's breast. On you I was cast from my birth, and since my mother bore me you have been my God. Do not be far from me, for trouble is near and there is no one to help. (9–11)

Both Jesus' actions and his words show us a tender, maternal side, and he uses a traditional image for God when he's clearly frustrated with the response of his own people. He says, "Jerusalem, Jerusalem, the city that kills the prophets and stones those who are sent to it! How often have I desired to gather your children together as a hen gathers her brood under her wings, and you were not willing!" (Matthew 23:37 and Luke 13:34). The image of God gathering us under her wings and sheltering us there is common in several psalms (17:8–9, 57:1–3, 61:4, and 91:4), and at times the mother bird is even an eagle, teaching the babies to fly by putting them on her wings and then letting them soar from there (Deuteronomy 32).

In Luke's gospel God is also imaged as a woman who is kneading bread, the job of the mother of the household: "And again he said, 'To what should I compare the kingdom of God? It is like yeast that a woman took and mixed in with three measures of flour until all of it was leavened'" (Luke 13:20–21 and Matthew 13:33).

And when Jesus is talking about God's delight at the return of someone who had strayed, he uses not only the image of a lost sheep, one familiar to men who were shepherds in his audience, but also an image familiar to women's experience as a housewife (and mother, we presume):

> Or what woman having ten silver coins, if she loses one of them, does not light a lamp, sweep the house, and search carefully until she finds it? When she has found it, she calls together her friends and neighbors, saying, "Rejoice with me, for I have found the coin that I had lost." Just so, I tell you, there is joy in the presence of the angels of God over one sinner who repents. (Luke 15:8–10)

Jesus then uses yet a third story on this theme of God's delight; he goes on to describe a father with an almost-foolish and mother-like tenderness in the story we usually refer to as the Prodigal Son.

Besides scripture, the notion of God as Mother also appears regularly in the writings of the Christian tradition as various figures reflect on their experience of faith. Early figures in the church such as Clement of Alexandria and Gregory of Nyssa comment on the maternal love of God. Margaret Hebbelthwaite, in her book *Motherhood and God*, quotes St. Gregory as he talks about how God communicates with us. "The divine power . . . is like a mother, compassionate to the inarticulate whimperings of her infants, who joins in their burblings . . ." (p. 131). The image he offers is one of God cooing and making baby talk to us as we try to express ourselves to Her!

Augustine of Hippo, one of the best known of the early Fathers of the church, commented to God, "Even when all is well with me, what am I but a creature suckled on your milk and feeding on yourself, the food that never perishes?" (Sanna, p. 27).

And in the Middle Ages St. Anselm talks about both God and St. Paul—through his ministry—as mothers:

> So you, Lord God, are the great mother.
> Then both of you are mothers.
> Even if you are fathers, you are also mothers.
> For you have brought it about that those born to death
> should be reborn to life—
> you by your own act, you by his power.
> (quoted in Hebbelthwaite, p. 132)

Interestingly, the image of God as mother and of devotion to Mary was especially strong around the twelfth century, especially among the Cistercian monks, leading them to see the role of the abbot as a nurturing, maternal one, as well.

St. Catherine of Siena, whom we discussed in the section on the season of Lent, in her mystical writings talked at times about "nursing at the breast of the crucified" and spoke of the Spirit as a mother who nurses us at the breast of divine charity. She also talks of Christ as our "foster mother."

St. Teresa of Avila, in the sixteenth century and whom we will explore in the section on Ordinary Time, talked about prayer as drinking and savoring the mother's milk of God without any words needing to be spoken. And Pope John XXIII, the gentle and jovial pope from a peasant background who called the Catholic Church to update itself through Vatican II, talks about God's love for him in his journal while still in the seminary:

> He took me, a country lad, from my home, and with the affection of a loving mother he has given me all I needed. I had nothing to eat and he provided food for me, I had nothing to wear and he clothed me, I had no books to study and he provided those also. At times I forgot him and he always gently recalled me. If my affection for him cooled, he warmed me in his breast, at the flame with which his Heart is always burning . . . and he still cares for me without respite, day and night, more than a mother cares for her child. (*Journal of a Soul*, pp. 90–91)

As powerful as these images of God as mother are, there are also some limitations to this way of thinking about God, as there are to any metaphor. Sallie McFague, in her essay "Mother God," cautions us, among other things, not to get too sentimental about God's motherhood and to realize that God as Mother is just one of many models we can use.

She also suggests three important implications to the notion of God as Mother: First, that since we are all "in God" as a child is in the womb and born from God, this can help give all of us an increased sense of the interdependence and inter-relatedness of all life. Second, since God the Mother nourishes each of us equally, the implications for justice—that all in our world must be fed—are clear. And third, as Mother, God wants us *all* to flourish. She explains:

> God is the mother of all existence, all beings, as well as the ecosystem that supports them, and while human parents tend to focus on our own species and specific individuals within that species, God as mother is impartial and inclusive as we can never be. The fulfilment of the entire created order, its growth and well-being, is the wish of the mother who brought it into being and who nurtures it. (Carr and Fiorenza 1989, p. 141)

As mothers continue to reflect on the process of nurturing their children, they find that their experience gives them an opportunity to "stand in God's shoes" just a bit and to glimpse a little of the amazing and tender love God has for each of us. God is indeed a loving Mother as well as a Father; let us hope that the years ahead will see the Christian community exploring more deeply what that means for all of us.

ANOINTING OF THE SICK: SACRAMENT OF HEALING

Whether we think of God as Mother or Father, we experience the Holy Spirit as a source of healing and of peace, qualities that are especially important at a time of serious illness or nearness to death. These times are important events in a family—and are often situations where mothers are deeply involved.

The sacrament of the Anointing of the Sick is a special way for the Church to be present at this time; this sacrament is based on Jesus' healing ministry toward the sick and also on the early Christian community's care for those who were ailing. We read in the letter of James, "Is anyone among you sick? He should summon the presbyters of the church, and they should pray over him and anoint (him) with oil in the name of the Lord, and the prayer of faith will save the sick person, and the Lord will raise him up" (5:14–15). Long before the advent of antibiotics and other modern medicines, oil was used for healing, both by drinking it and anointing with it—rubbing it on the skin, as we saw in the Christmas/Epiphany section.

Although between the medieval period and the late 1960s the Anointing of the Sick was called "Extreme Unction" and was reserved for those in danger of death, this sacrament has now been restored to its earlier role as a special blessing at any time of serious illness. When someone is ill, she can often feel isolated, alone, and scared by what she is facing. The sacrament of Anointing helps that individual to know the support and care of the community of faith, as well as of God, at a time of suffering.

Not only does the person who is ill need the community's support, she can also have an important ministry and role within the community, praying for the rest of the church and supporting them in this way. Fr. Richard Fragoumeni, in his book *Come to the Feast: An Introduction to Eucharistic Transformation*, comments on another aspect to the role of the sick within the community of faith:

We see in the sick and suffering a witness to their ability to see the overwhelming gift of God in the absence of the usual support. They plunge into suffering and come up with new insights into who God is and what life is about, and they emerge more grateful for life. That's the paradox. We anoint them because they are prophets. Anointing the sick is a prophetic anointing. We anoint the sick as if they were Christ on the cross. They are to be a sign for the church that even when they are in the desert with only stones to eat, they are grateful, they know a presence of God in an absence. (p. 55)

The Anointing of the Sick is also a powerful way to remember the Spirit's presence in the midst of the community. In the sacrament, as the priest anoints the forehead of the sick person, he says, "Through this holy anointing may the Lord in his love and mercy help you through the grace of the Holy Spirit." This ritual, of course, needs to be linked to the larger picture of the Church's pastoral care of those who are sick— pastoral care in which women are increasingly involved, both in hospitals and in parishes.

As a culture we are becoming increasingly aware of how true healing needs to include the *whole* person, much like the incarnational quality to mothers' spirituality that we discussed in the Christmas section. As mothers, we know that physical healing is deeply connected to the emotional and spiritual aspects of who we are, from the kissing of children's "owies" to the healing of bodies and minds in all kinds of ways in which mothers are involved, both at home and in their professional roles. Mothers are often aware of the importance of massage and healing touch as key ways to care for hurting persons. As we as mothers work to care for and heal others, we often find that *we* are healed as well, and we are more aware of the Spirit's powerful comforting presence and peace.

MOTHERS SPEAK

This time we hear from mothers and their experience as it relates to the wisdom they have found:

Being a mother is the most important thing you'll ever do, so let it become your priority. Make life changes if necessary. Create a support system and accept, ask for, and even pay for help. Read, eat well, find ways to really rest and relax and to simplify your life. Trust your instincts, but also look for people whose parenting style you admire and learn from them. Get time away—alone and with your spouse. Look for the humor in situations. Be affectionate and honest with your children. Don't break their spirits! Get help for your own anger and emotional issues and find healthy ways to honor your needs for prayer, exercise, etc.

Take time to really listen to your children. Sit down with them, be present, give them your full attention, be open, accepting, validate them. These are precious moments that you can share lovingly with your children.

Keep a journal and revisit it. Don't get hung up with making frequent entries; that may only frustrate you. When significant moments or thoughts come, sit with them, jot them down, and go back to the memories as often as time allows.

Don't be too quick to rescue your children from their mistakes. Let them experience the natural or logical consequences of their actions when they are young and stakes are low (like not rushing the forgotten lunch or permission slip to school). It's a lot harder when they get older and the stakes might be more serious, have lifelong consequences, or even result in death (like sexual promiscuity, drinking, drugs, etc.)

The one thing I would tell new mothers is not to be afraid. If you love your child, truly love your child, then most of the mistakes you make along the way will amount to nothing in the end. Whether you nurse or feed by bottle, whether you work outside the home or stay at home, whether you are an authoritarian/autocratic/laissez-faire parent, there is no perfect formula for any one family. The key is to be the best you—or at least growing toward the best you—and to love your child with all your heart.

[My mother] let us be kids and do what kids tend to do, like jumping on the bed. Her philosophy was that we wouldn't get new furniture until we could sit. Besides, we wouldn't jump on the bed for the rest of our lives. She had an incredible level of patience that allowed her to let us make mistakes, some quite painful, and she was there when we most needed her—after we realized the consequences of our actions. She did step in if it concerned life and death. She didn't try to pretend she had all the answers herself, and she admitted when she was wrong.

Children need many mothers; you cannot and will not be able to be everything to them. Look for and nurture wise and good "other mothers" for your children, and be willing to do the same for another.

All women (including moms) need women friends; make time for friendship, for friendship is a sacred and holy place that is necessary for living a sacramental life.

MODELS FROM THE TRADITION

When we look to the saints and others for models of the wisdom and wonder within mothers' spirituality, St. Paula,

Blessed Julian of Norwich, and Sr. Thea Bowman are three women who come to mind.

St. Paula (347–404) was a wealthy Roman wife and mother whose life seemed shattered with the death of her husband. However, she found a group of women trying to live the spirit of the gospel message in the city of Rome, and through them she met St. Jerome, whom she was to befriend and support.

Jerome was a prickly personality, difficult for most people to get along with, and an important early Christian scholar who later translated the Bible into Latin from its original languages. He was impressed with Paula's curiosity about scripture, her intelligence, and her facility with languages. She already knew Greek and Latin, and she learned Hebrew from Jerome more quickly and easily than he himself had done.

When Jerome moved to the Holy Land—in part because of malicious rumors about him and Paula—she and her daughter Eustochium followed and visited many holy sites, helping found two monasteries and assisting Jerome with his studies. She was buried there in the Holy Land, and her epitaph, written by St. Jerome, says in part, ". . . she preferred the poverty of Christ and the humble fields of Bethlehem to the splendours of Rome" (Jones, *Women Saints*, p. 85).

St. Paula reminds mothers of our intelligence and the need to fill our minds as well as our hearts, both for ourselves but also for our daughters and sons to see that women hunger to learn about our faith and about the world in which we live.

Blessed Julian of Norwich (1342–1416) wrote more completely and powerfully on the motherhood of God and Jesus than probably anyone else in the Christian tradition. Like the woman who raised Hildegard of Bingen, whom we saw in the section on Christmas/Epiphany, she was an anchoress, a hermit connected to the local church in Norwich, England. In *Showings, or Revelations of Divine Love*, her account of her mystical experiences, she gives us a striking sense of God's motherhood, especially describing Jesus as our Mother. Here we sense her understanding of the Trinity:

> I understand three ways of contemplating motherhood in God. The first is the foundation of our nature's creation; the second is his taking of our nature, where the motherhood of grace begins; the third is the motherhood at work. And in that, by the same grace, everything is penetrated, in length and in breadth, in height and in depth without end; and it is all one love. (Colledge and Walsh, p. 297)

Julian of Norwich reminds us of the simple yet powerful relationship we have with God, especially as mothers, a God whose love is far more like our own than we sometimes imagine.

Sr. Thea Bowman, FSPA (1937–1990) lived in a completely different time and culture—the twentieth century in the United States—and yet she showed the same energy of the Holy Spirit at work. Sr. Thea was a gifted teacher and storyteller, always inviting her listeners to get actively involved with the joy of the gospel message.

She became a Catholic while attending a parochial school at the age of ten, and she went on to eventually found the Institute of Black Catholic Studies at Xavier University in New Orleans and to help African Americans and the rest of the church to appreciate more clearly the gifts of Black Catholics within the Church.

> In one speech she noted that women were not allowed to preach in the Catholic church. But this shouldn't stop them from preaching everywhere else! "God has called to us to

speak the word that is Christ, that is truth, that is salvation. And if we speak that word in love and faith, with patience and prayer and perseverance, it will take root. It does have power to save us. Call one another! Testify! Teach! Act on the Word! Witness!" (Ellsburg, p. 143)

She addressed many groups, including the U.S. Catholic Bishops at their annual meeting in 1989; by this time she knew she was dying of breast cancer, but even from a wheelchair she embodied the joy, strength, and hope so strong in the Negro spirituals. In her final months and years, she said her prayer had become, "Lord, let me live until I die."

In her life, as well as in her death, Sr. Thea reminded all of us of the energy of the Spirit which calls us to use all our gifts, our culture, and our lives to share God's joy and peace with those around us.

SCRIPTURE FOR REFLECTION

As we reflect on our own lives as mothers and the experience of the wisdom of the Spirit in our spirituality, the following passages may be helpful, in addition to the passages mentioned above. Please try to take some time with one or more of them and with the questions that follow. You may prefer to reflect on these with other mothers. Wisdom speaks:

The LORD created me at the beginning of his work, the first of his acts of long ago. Ages ago I was set up, at the first, before the beginning of the earth. When there were no depths I was brought forth, when there were no springs abounding with water. Before the mountains had been shaped, before the hills, I was brought forth—when he had not yet made earth and fields, or the world's first bits of soil.

When he established the heavens, I was there, when he drew a circle on the face of the deep, when he made firm the skies above, when he established the fountains of the deep, when he assigned to the sea its limit, so that the waters might not transgress his command, when he marked out the foundations of the earth, then I was beside him, like a master worker; and I was daily his delight, rejoicing before him always, rejoicing in his inhabited world and delighting in the human race. And now, my children, listen to me: happy are those who keep my ways. (Proverbs 8:22–33)

—*How do you experience wisdom in your life as a quality of and from God? How do you see it at work in yourself or in others?*
—*How do you experience wisdom in your delight and wonder at all of creation? What is your strongest experience of this lately?*

Sing for joy, O heavens, and exult, O earth; break forth, O mountains, into singing! For the LORD has comforted his people, and will have compassion on his suffering ones. But Zion said, "The LORD has forsaken me, my Lord has forgotten me." Can a woman forget her nursing child, or show no compassion for the child of her womb? Even these may forget, yet I will not forget you. See, I have inscribed you on the palms of my hands; your walls are continually before me. (Isaiah 49:13–16)

—*Try to imagine forgetting one of your children and see how impossible that is. Does that help your prayer when you feel abandoned by God?*
—*Can you picture God's "hands," either holding you or with your name written upon them? Does that image help you understand your relationship with God?*
—*Listen to God tell you, "I will never forget you." What do you say to in response to God?*

The prophet Isaiah shows God as a midwife helping Jerusalem give birth:

Before she was in labor she gave birth; before her pain came upon her she delivered a son. Who has heard of such a thing? Who has seen such things? Shall a land be born in one day? Shall a nation be delivered in one moment? Yet as soon as Zion was in labor she delivered her children.

Shall I open the womb and not deliver? says the LORD; shall I, the one who delivers, shut the womb? says your God. Rejoice with Jerusalem, and be glad for her, all you who love her; rejoice with her in joy, all you who mourn over her—that you may nurse and be satisfied from her consoling breast; that you may drink deeply with delight from her glorious bosom.

For thus says the LORD: I will extend prosperity to her like a river, and the wealth of the nations like an overflowing stream; and you shall nurse and be carried on her arm, and dandled on her knees. As a mother comforts her child, so I will comfort you; you shall be comforted in Jerusalem. (Isaiah 66:7–13)

—*What is the "midwife God" helping you to "give birth to" in your life?*
—*How are you comforted by God? Is the image of God as mother or midwife helpful to your relationship of faith? How?*

Other Scripture Passages to Explore

Ezekiel 37:1–14—The Spirit gives new life to dry bones.

Luke 13:10–17—Jesus heals a woman bent over with worries and pain.

1 Kings 3:11–28—King Solomon shows his wisdom in a dispute between two mothers.

Questions for Individual or Group Reflection

Which of the gifts of the Holy Spirit—wisdom, understanding, counsel, fortitude, knowledge, piety, fear of the
Lord—have you seen in yourself or in someone else? How
have you seen it at work?

What gift does each child of yours call forth from you? What
experiences have caused those gifts to be "opened" or used?

Have you had an experience of inspiration or creativity or
understanding across differences that is evidence of the
Spirit at work in your life?

Is the image of the Trinity as a community of friends, perhaps involved in a dance without beginning or end, helpful
to your faith?

Have you ever blessed your children? If so, how was that experience, and if not, is that something you might consider doing?

Resources for This Season

*The following are some resources related to the themes explored here; full
information on these can be found at the end of this book.*

Carr and Fiorenza, *Motherhood: Experience, Institution, Theology*
Colledge and Walsh, *Julian of Norwich: Showings*
Cunneen, *Mother Church*
M. Finley, *The Seven Gifts of the Holy Spirit*
Fischer, *Autumn Gospel*
Hebbelthwaite, *Motherhood and God*
Sanna, *Motherhood: A Spiritual Journey*

Chapter Six

ORDINARY TIME
Living Motherhood Day to Day

DONNA LOOKED IN ON HER CHILDREN ONCE MORE before she crawled into bed herself. It had certainly been a busy day—getting everyone out the door this morning, dropping the older two kids at school and the youngest at the day care center, putting in a few hours at her part-time job, picking the kids up again and taking them to the park for a chance to enjoy the beautiful weather for a little while, then running a couple errands that she needed to do. After they got home, it was time to try to get some dinner on the table and spend some time with Jim after dinner while the kids watched TV and did homework, and, finally, to get everyone off to bed with his help.

There were so many sights and sounds packed into the day, as she thought about it now, that it was almost overwhelming. She was grateful for so many gifts in her life and for her ability to handle all that she had to deal with right now. "Please, loving God," she thought, "help me to see You a bit more clearly in my busy life."

Donna's days are not unlike those of many mothers, women who are juggling many tasks in the course of a day.

The season of Ordinary Time gives us the opportunity to look at how we mothers spend our time, day after day, and how God is a part of that—whether we are aware of it or not.

WHAT IS THIS SEASON?

Ordinary Time technically includes not only the time after Pentecost until the First Sunday of Advent, but also those Sundays between Epiphany and the beginning of Lent. We, however, will focus on the time after the season of Pentecost. This season is called "Ordinary," not because it is not extraordinary, but because these Sundays and weeks are *ordered*, numbered one after another, as in "The Twelfth Sunday in Ordinary Time." This is the time in the church year to explore how Christians live out their lives day after day, from the time after the Spirit's coming at Pentecost until the end of time, a prospect which we recall on the feast of Christ the King, the last Sunday of Ordinary Time.

FROM THE TRADITION

When we consider how we live our lives day after day during Ordinary Time, one topic that arises is the norms or principles by which we live. As Christians, not only do we try to live by the Ten Commandments from our Jewish heritage, but we also want to follow Jesus as he deepened those values by how he lived and what he taught. Let us explore both of these in light of mothers' experience.

The **Ten Commandments**, or Decalogue, spell out how God calls the Israelite people to live with one another in light of the covenant, or relationship in faith, that they have with God. These commandments are short and direct, making clear what God expects of all of us. Let us consider each one briefly and some of its implications for mothers:

1. *I am the Lord your God; you shall not have strange gods before me.* (You are not God; I am. And your children are mine first; I will take care of them even when you cannot.)

2. *You shall not take the name of the Lord your God in vain.* (I am a part of every aspect of your life; when you look for me and speak of me, I'll be there. And your children will learn of me by watching your example.)

3. *Remember to keep holy the Lord's day.* (When you take time for me in your life and nurture yourself so that you can remember my love for you, you will be able to give to others out of that abundance.)

4. *Honor your father and your mother.* (Respect those who have nurtured and taught you; they have shared my love with you.)

5. *You shall not kill.* (Be gentle and kind to others, even when it is most difficult.)

6. *You shall not commit adultery.* (Your faithful love and healthy regard for the gift of your sexuality are important ways to embody my love.)

7. *You shall not steal.* (Remember what is truly important in your life and that possessions are secondary.)

8. *You shall not bear false witness against your neighbor.* (Speak well of others and do not judge them unfairly.)

9, 10. *You shall not covet your neighbor's wife or goods.* (Don't waste your energy in envying others or their possessions.)

Besides the guidance of the Commandments, which Jesus summed up in just two when asked—first, love God with all your heart, your soul, your mind, and your strength, and second, love your neighbor as yourself—Jesus showed us a powerful way of being a caring presence for everyone. He seemed to draw others to him, especially those who were in need or on the outskirts of society, but this also made the religious officials of his time uncomfortable, in part because his actions made them look bad.

As we try to follow Jesus' example of care for others, some of the possible ways to do that are spelled out in the **spiritual and corporal works of mercy**, a list based partly on the Last Judgment in Matthew's gospel, chapter 25. The corporal works of mercy are to: feed the hungry, give drink to the thirsty, clothe the naked, shelter the homeless, visit the sick, visit the imprisoned, and bury the dead. The spiritual works of mercy are somewhat parallel to these and reflect the practice of Christians throughout the centuries: to counsel the doubtful, instruct the ignorant, admonish the sinner, comfort the sorrowful, forgive injuries, bear wrongs patiently, and pray for the living and the dead. These works of mercy certainly sound worthwhile, and most mothers will probably feel guilty for not doing more of them. But at the same time mothers also know that they don't really have the *time* to do much more in their daily lives, as much as they would like to.

Kathleen Chesto, in her essay, "On the Judgment," reminds us that these works of mercy are more present than we know, right before our eyes—so close that we usually miss them:

 I have a vision. It is all of us standing before the Lord on judgment day. And the Lord will say: "I was hungry, and you fed me, thirsty, and you gave me a drink, naked and you clothed me, homeless and you sheltered me, imprisoned and you visited me . . ." (Matthew 25:36)

Puzzled, we'll respond:

"When, Lord, when did I see you hungry?"

And the Lord will say:

"How could you ask? You of the three and a half million peanut butter and jelly sandwiches, how could you even ask?"

"But thirsty, Lord?"

"I was in the Kool-Aide line that came in with the summer heat and the flies and left mud on your floor and finger prints on your walls and you gave me a drink."

"Naked, Lord? Homeless?"

"I was born to you naked and homeless and you sheltered me, first in wombs and then in arms and clothed me with your love. And you spent the next twenty years keeping me in jeans."

"But imprisoned, Lord? I didn't visit you in a prison. I was never in a prison."

"Oh, yes, for I was imprisoned in my littleness, behind the bars of a crib and I cried out in the night and you came. I was imprisoned inside an eleven-year-old body that was bursting with so many new emotions I didn't know who I was and you loved me into being myself. And I was imprisoned behind my teenage rebellion, my anger, and my stereo set, and you waited outside my locked door for me to let you in.

"Now, beloved, enter into the joy which has been prepared for you from all eternity."

Amen. (pp. 29–30)

The face of Christ *is* right before our eyes, which—paradoxically—is probably the reason we can't see it all that often.

In order to begin to see some of the ways that God may be right before our eyes but easily missed, mothers know that they need regular times of **prayer**. However, mothers also find that, like Donna in the example that began this season, it's hard to find much time or energy for formal prayers in the course of their busy days. What *is* prayer, and how can Catholic traditions of prayer help mothers to see where prayer weaves into their busy days?

Prayer has been defined in many ways, but at its root it is really *being present to God*, in much the same way that we are present to others in our lives, day in and day out. There are many approaches to prayer—almost as many as there are kinds of people—but all of them strive to help the individual to be more aware of God's *presence* and God's *presents* in that person's life. Prayer can either be alone or with others. First, we will examine some of the more public forms of prayer within the Catholic tradition to see what light they can help shed on prayer in a mother's life and experience, and then we will explore personal prayer for mothers a bit further.

Although Christians don't pray five times a day as Muslims do, they have developed some very definite public forms of prayer through the centuries—other than the liturgy of the Eucharist, which we already have explored. A primary public prayer of the Church from the early centuries has been the **Liturgy of the Hours**, also called the Divine Office.

The earliest Christians gathered to continue the prayer of the Temple and Synagogue, in which they had participated, as had Jesus. There is evidence that many of them probably met in the morning to greet the new day, at midday, and again at evening to give thanks for the day and to ask pardon for failings during it and for protection through the coming night.

This gradually evolved into the medieval pattern of monastic prayer, with eight times of prayer a day: vespers (at the end of the working day), compline (before bedtime), matins (in the middle of the night), lauds (at daybreak), prime (early morning), terce (middle of the morning), sext (at noon), and none (in the middle of the afternoon.) Some of these prayers were much longer than others, but each of them usually involved singing hymns, reciting psalms and canticles, and at least one reading and response.

These times of prayer were beautiful, but the time they took each day was not practical for lay Christians, who weren't part of a religious community or ordained. Gradually these public prayers became primarily for priests and religious who didn't have families to provide for. One of the effects of the widening gap between the two sets of Christians—the laity on the one hand, and priests and religious on the other, was that those who couldn't read or spend as much time at church turned to private devotions to nourish their faith, including the practice of saying 150 Our Fathers daily instead of the 150 psalms, usually by saying 50 at a time.

Saying the Lord's Prayer gradually was replaced by the Hail Mary, in honor of Mary, to whom there was a particularly strong devotion in the medieval era. The result became the **rosary**, complete with the use of beads or knots to count the prayers while meditating on events in the life of Jesus and Mary, a practice that was especially promoted by St. Dominic and his followers. The rosary has been an important Catholic form of prayer, with ten Hail Marys said for each of the five Joyful, five Sorrowful, and five Glorious mysteries of the rosary—usually only one of which is used at a time. Pope John Paul II has recently added the five Luminous mysteries, which offer even more aspects of the gospel to consider in prayer.

One other form of public prayer that has emerged in the Catholic tradition is that of a **litany**, especially the Litany of the Saints. Litanies are usually prayers for help with a series of petitions to which those gathered respond, for example, "Pray for us." This form was especially popular in the Middle Ages, but its roots reach back into ancient religions and Jewish worship.

What do the Liturgy of the Hours, the rosary, and litanies have to say to mothers' experiences of prayer today? First of all, we know that different times of the day have different needs and give a different focus to our thoughts and prayers; our energy as we begin the day is usually different from the way we end the day.

We often begin with hopes for the new day and gratitude for the gift of it, even if there's a lot to be done. The name of the traditional morning prayer, "Lauds," comes from the Latin word for "praise," and that is often what the new day calls us to do.

The middle of the day may bring a respite at naptime or a lunch break, something that allows us to remember God's presence in the midst of what we are doing.

The end of the day, as we tuck our children in for the night after the bedtime rituals, is a naturally reflective time. Our children sense this, too, and usually seize the chance to ask us anything from the most random to the most thoughtful questions—usually when we most want to sit by ourselves quietly for a few moments! This is a time to review the day, as we come to the end of it in gratitude and even to ask for safety through the night, much as a small child might ask for our reassuring presence.

And if we end up being awakened in the middle of the night to feed an infant, tend to a sick child, or just to give a drink or give comfort after a scary dream, we have our own time of Matins, of presence to our God in the middle of the night.

As our family changes, the unique rhythm of our lives changes, so that the challenge of finding the spaces where a bit of prayer and reflection might be "tucked in" changes. But no matter when or where that is, we know our God is there, waiting for us. Mothers' prayer—no matter when it happens—is often prayer on the run, or at least in the moment.

Many of the traditional forms for prayer assume a process of quiet and withdrawal from the busyness of daily chores in order to center and focus on God's presence in one's life, a quiet and space that is usually not possible for mothers. But the rosary helps remind us that prayer is *of the heart*.

Much like saying the prayers again and again while meditating on the mysteries of the gospel, we are called—in the midst of much busyness—to recall the deeper dimension of what is before us. Indeed, we have our own "mysteries"—joyful, sorrowful, glorious, and even luminous some days. For some mothers that may look like saying a decade of the rosary for each member of her family or praying for a different child each day of the week. For other, busier moms, it may look like breathing a quick prayer of thanks or asking for help in the midst of what she is doing—whenever she thinks of it. This is the kind of prayer—taking what is before us to God in prayer—which we see in the gospels when Mary "ponders all these things in her heart," as we have mentioned before.

And the tradition of litanies, especially the Litany of the Saints, reminds us that we can call on all kinds of help and support—"pray for us"—from those living and dead, as we try to do the best job we can of being God's love in our children's lives and in the world.

Our children can also teach us, their mothers, about prayer at times. When they were preschoolers, our children taught me a lot about how they needed to pray and celebrate—from having a marching parade complete with "rhythm instruments" from the kitchen for a Palm Sunday procession celebrating Jesus' entry into Jerusalem to a simple Way of the Cross experience with a cross of two sticks and "props" from the toy box and the kitchen. We even had a blessing of their riding toys one day after our middle son got a new tricycle. Whether it was their nightly blessing before going to sleep or the blessing they would give us before we traveled, they taught me how much their faith needed to be a part of their everyday lives and to involve their bodies.

And the depth of good theology that children can handle is reflected for me in a prayer about faith, hope, and love that a second grader wrote in a religious education class my friend was teaching: "Dear God, I believe in you because I exist, I trust in you because night turns to day, and I love you because you are God." Not bad.

One way that traditional Catholic piety has imaged God's care for each of us, especially as children, is the tradition of a **guardian angel**—that we each have a special messenger from God assigned to watch over us. While never defined as dogma, this has been a comforting way for mothers to entrust their children into God's care. And Jesus seem to refer to this idea in Matthew's gospel when he says, "See that you do not despise one of these little ones, for I say to you that their angels in heaven always look upon the face of my heavenly Father" (Matthew 18:10).

Mary Lynn Hendrickson suggests a variation on the traditional prayer to a Guardian Angel for parents in these troubled times:

> Angel of God, (their/his/her) guardian dear,
> please take to heart this parent's fear.
> Ever this day, be at (their/his/her) side;
> in your embrace, let (them/him/her) abide.[1]

Guardian angels are remembered in the liturgy on October 2, which falls during Ordinary Time.

Another feast that falls within the season of Ordinary Time is that of the **Assumption of Mary**, celebrated on August 15, which honors Mary as she was taken up into heaven body and soul, without having suffered the corruption of death. When Pope Pius XII declared this a dogma in

---

1. Reprinted with permission from "Weekly Meditations for Busy Parents," a free service of *At Home with Our Faith* newsletter, sponsored by the Claretian Missionaries: www.homefaith.com, 1-800-328-6515.

1950, after it had been a part of Catholic belief for centuries, some reactions were mixed, but Gertrud Mueller Nelson suggests how important this belief really is:

> . . . Carl Jung, the Swiss Protestant psychiatrist, responded promptly [at the time], saying that the proclamation of Mary's bodily assumption into heaven was the most important religious event since the Reformation. Jung, with his deep respect for the symbolic life, with his skillful and creative imagination, could hear and see the symbol that the Pope was offering humankind. He indicated that this was the beginning of a new age—that now things would begin to happen.
>
> For, while the Pope with this proclamation was responding to the growing popular devotion to Mary, he was also giving us, whether he was aware of it or not, a powerful, poetic image that emerged out of the Church's own soul or dream life. . . . Mary, the archetypal feminine, once queen of all that was earthy, dark, unconscious, and frightfully fruitful, she who had been left to the darkness, where all that is feminine is feared or honored, served or oppressed—symbolically and literally—must now be raised into the light of our new understanding. (p. 200)

This glorious feast of Mary happens in the middle of August, at the peak of the season when the earth is most fruitful and the "feminine" need to respect the earth and all that is natural is so clearly before us. This is indeed a time to bless and enjoy the fruits of the garden and to be aware of the ways that feminine energy is at work in our lives and in our world.

As the liturgical year comes to an end in mid-November and prepares to begin again with Advent, the scripture readings ask us to consider the **last things** at the end of time. Although theologians have speculated since the middle ages and before—as have we all—about heaven and hell, death and judgment, we still have little that we can say with much certainty.

When we're asked if a child's dead pet is now in heaven and what it's like there, we're up against mystery. We *do* know that after death we will be with God—unless we have consistently chosen to reject God and to embrace selfishness and sin, which we don't know if anyone has ever done. We also believe that the choices we make *now* are the beginnings of what we will experience more fully after death, so that heaven is something we begin to experience *now*, not just after we've died.

Although we can let our imaginations run wild—and have—about what things might look like after we die, we don't have very much clear "information" about *eschatology*, the study of the last things. But the last Sunday of Ordinary Time, the feast of Christ The King, reminds us each year that Jesus is King and Leader over *all* peoples. He is even Lord over all notions that we may have of "how things should be"—the Kingdom or reign of God—because his love and care goes beyond what we can even imagine.

As mothers, in our daily tasks we focus both on very immediate concerns and needs *and* on the eventual outcome of whatever our children are about; we intuitively keep our eyes on the "last" and most important "things" while we are dealing with a lot of specific issues of care. And every once in a while—when we least expect it—we may catch a glimpse of heaven, right before our eyes.

MOTHERS' SPIRITUALITY
IS *EMOTIONALLY INTEGRATED*

As mothers live their lives day in and day out, their spirituality has a strong component of heart *and* head, of feelings as well as intellect and reason. Author Sally Cunneen was struck by the blend of both after asking many women about their experiences in the mid 1960s. She comments: "Like the connected knowers that women psychologists have discovered mature women thinkers to be, they thought about what they cared about and cared about how they thought" (p. 20). Sometimes this combination can be called "reflective feeling," or it may show itself in women's intuition; we just *know* something, and it is a knowing of our feelings *and* our intellect.

In her fascinating book *Maternal Thinking*, Sara Ruddick comments on how much our feelings are part of the information that we mothers use every day.

> In protecting her child, a mother is besieged by feeling, her own and her children's. She is dependent on these feelings to interpret the world. The world that mothers and children see and name, separately and together, is constructed by feeling. Objects, events, people, and feelings themselves are selected and given meaning in terms of emotional stories: Watch out for this "this," "this" is what or who I hate; "this" is the fearful place/person; "this" can be approached, should be hugged close. A mother's angry, fearful, or solicitous responses to her children are often her best clue to the meaning of the actions that evoked the emotions. Even more clearly, a child's emotional expressions, however difficult they may be for a mother to witness, are essential to the understanding that makes protection possible. (p. 69)

Ruddick even observes that anything that significantly relieves or blunts these feelings for a mother—substance abuse comes to mind—could inhibit her ability as a mother.

If, as these authors point out, we are not only "feelers," but "connected knowers," for whom emotional information is key, how does this affect our spirituality? One way that this shows itself is our focus on empathy, on how a situation feels for the other person; we tend to ask, and encourage our children to ask, "How did that make the other person feel?" We see this element of empathy in the gospels in the woman who anoints Jesus, who seems to be one of the few people who is able to *feel* what lies ahead for him.

This integration of feeling within our spirituality is also linked to our need as mothers to be specific and practical, to use images, examples, and stories, even poetry at times to illustrate our faith. We often want to use these means to draw from our experience first and *then* look at what our religious tradition has to say to that experience. As mothers we also can tend to be more aware of the setting and surroundings for our prayer than men, knowing that what our senses tell us affects our whole selves. And we want to look at the practical implications of our beliefs, the *so-what* questions, to see what difference this will make in how we live each day. We can tend to be impatient when spirituality gets too theoretical and abstracted from daily reality.

These practical qualities are, in turn, strongly linked to what Sara Ruddick calls mothers' protective work. She comments, "In protective work, feeling, thinking, and action are conceptually linked; feelings demand reflection, which is in turn tested by action, which is in turn tested by the feelings it provokes" (p. 70). This important component of motherhood changes as our children start to grow, as she explains:

> Somebody must be alert for things that go wrong and be ready to set them right and get help. . . . Soon the stairs have to be barricaded. The lethal tools of household work, from needles to cleaners to glue, will be locked away. Mild medicines can turn poisonous if a child mistakes them for candy. A mother has to childproof her home, but she cannot childproof her city or farm. A child has to be taught general strategies of safety so that she can protect herself from dangers

when she is outside her mother's domain where it sometimes seems that there is no limit to risks the world offers. (p. 71)

Not only does a mother need to have the habit in a child's early years of what Ruddick calls "scrutinizing," scanning a situation for potential hazards, but we mothers also need to have a sense of humility that we can't protect our children from everything—nor do we want to; this is linked to the letting go that we explored in the season of Lent.

Mothers bring all this to their relationship with God: a close link to their feelings and intuition, a pragmatic focus, and a need for practical examples and the consequences of everyday situations. In Jesus they find someone who is deeply feeling as well as a decisive thinker, who often uses specific examples in his parables and stories and who shows by his example the consequences of following his teachings.

As we come to God in prayer or watch for our children's safety, feelings are indeed an important part of mothers' spirituality—not *instead of* or *apart from* thinking and reflection, but as a part of those important functions.

ACHIEVING A BALANCE

How can this integration of feeling and thinking be out of balance at times in mothers? One common imbalance in mothers is to only acknowledge and discuss the "positive" feelings that we have, while denying some of the other feelings that are there, because they don't seem like ones that a mother should have. Cunneen warns:

> . . . the extreme intimacy of the mother–child relationship means that powerful negative feelings will emerge and must

be acknowledged and dealt with. The mother who thinks her role is always to be "good" will find it very difficult to acknowledge her anger and frustration because she "isn't supposed" to have such feelings. She will waste her time repressing her feelings—which are important signs to which she should pay attention—instead of learning how to deal with the situations that cause them. (p. 84)

And Sara Ruddick further reminds us, "What we are pleased to call 'mother-love' is intermixed with hate, sorrow, impatience, resentment, and despair; thought-provoking ambivalence is a hallmark of mothering" (p. 68).

Sometimes we need the "experts" to reassure us that it is perfectly normal to have such a range of feelings as mothers. The question is what we *do* with those feelings and whether we can learn from what they have to teach us. Can we acknowledge them to ourselves and—if appropriate—to our children and then deal with them constructively, deciding—perhaps together—what to do about the situation that prompted those feelings?

Another way to be out of balance is that sometimes mothers can *overfocus* on their emotions in their spirituality and not integrate them well with the rest of who they are, forgetting to include the reasoning part of themselves. They can then end up with what I call "sentimental piety," a faith which is deeply feeling and/or cute but which may not really challenge them to change or grow.

STORIES: A MOTHER'S TOOL

Change and growth *are* constants in motherhood; in order to cope with and understand this ever-changing "terrain," mothers often use storytelling. The stories that we share in our families are a rich, often-overlooked resource of who we are and who God is in our midst. Although these stories may not seem in any way religious at first glance, in a sense they are our own *scripture*, our Liturgy of the Word. Whenever we gather and tell the stories, we hear again the unique way that God is at work in the midst of our family.

"Tell us about the time. . . ." "Remember when. . . ." And the stories come tumbling out: about mom and dad's honeymoon, about the time we took that vacation and stayed in that strange place, about when Uncle John got hurt on the camping trip. Sometimes we only realize what some of our stories are when we have the opportunity to tell them to someone who hasn't heard them all before. Suddenly we hear about all the holy times, the holy places, the holy people in our midst. These stories are certainly not all about the *pleasant* times; there are plenty of tragedies lurking in most families. In fact, some of the most interesting stories may be the carefully kept secrets—the ones that few, if any, know.

Within these family stories, which hold an amazing amount of power as well as information, are stories that mothers tell and use in a unique way. Ruddick points out that these anecdotes help us to refine our concrete, attentive ways of knowing:

> In their storytelling, mothers share and elaborate their ob-servations, making a coherent, often amusing, dramatic, or poignant story of their children's particularities. Individu-ally and collectively, they rehearse their judgments and es-tablish continuities in their ongoing nurturing activities. Ideally, a mother's stories are as beneficial to her children as they are to her. As she pieces her children's days together, a mother creates for herself and her children the confidence that the children have a life, very much their own and inex-tricably connected with others. (p. 98)

Our stories for our children begin with the accounts of being pregnant with them and their birth or their adoption. Our children love to hear the stories of how they began, stories which begin to shape them in lasting ways. Besides stories, there are also the songs and music we have shared with our children, starting with lullabies to them when they were infants; many musicians—and the rest of us—can trace their love of music back to their mothers.

A key part of our role as mothers is to help hold our children's memories and stories. That act of *re-membering* helps us recall *again* that we are indeed *members* of one another—in our families and beyond. Mothers do this in many ways, in baby books or albums; one way I tried to do it was by keeping a journal for each of our sons and then giving it to each one when he graduated from high school. At times the entries were a year or two apart—despite my best intentions—but I finally realized that whatever, and whenever, I wrote there would be precious for them later.

Ruddick says our stories as mothers need to have three qualities to them: realism, compassion, and delight. They need to be *realistic* enough that the child can trust the truthfulness of the maternal narrator; while there may be occasional situations that call for some editing, we need to be careful to not leave out the "negative" parts of our stories. And when our stories are *compassionate*, we are generous toward the faults that come to light, which can lead the child who is listening to be similarly generous toward himself or others. Mothers' stories easily have the component of *delight* when we're talking about our own children, but the differences between children and our expectations for each child can present significant challenges for us at times.

Sharing these stories—with their realism, compassion, and delight—with other mothers is an important social task, one that can too easily get lost in the increased pace of our lives. Telling our stories can also help us to realize when some of the challenges that we are watching our children face may bring up old fears and concerns *within us* that we've kept deeply buried. Sometimes the most helpful and healing thing we can do for our children is to admit to them *our own* fears—perhaps from when we were just their age.

Change is not limited to our children, of course; there is a very real sense in which each of our children has a different mother, not only in the sense of different memories because of their unique perspective but also because *we* are changing and growing—and hopefully learning—as we gain more experience and hopefully more wisdom as moms. And part of that growth may be to realize that *we in turn were once mothered*—that is, that we were dependent on someone's nurturing love, just as our children now are dependent on ours. This is both humbling and wonderful to consider: None of us is really as self-made as we may want to think in our culture, and our life itself is a pure gift.

THE DOMESTIC CHURCH AND HOSPITALITY: THE HOLINESS OF HOME

The stories that we tell about our children and our families point to a key aspect of our daily lives in Ordinary Time: the holiness of what happens in our homes. The awareness of our families as the basic unit of the church—in the sense of a gathering of believers—is an ancient idea that has been rediscovered in recent years. As the U.S. bishops put it in their pastoral message, *Follow the Way of Love*, issued to families in November 1993:

> A family is our first community and the most basic way in which the Lord gathers us, forms us, and acts in the world. The early church expressed this truth by calling the Christian family a domestic church or church of the home. . . . The point of the teaching is simple, yet profound. As Christian families, you not only belong to the Church, but your daily life is a true expression of the Church. (p. 8)

After enumerating a number of ways in which families live out the mission of the church in the home—including loving and serving one another and others, forgiving and celebrating life—the bishops add that no family does all of this perfectly, and neither does any parish or diocesan church. Then they add, "But remember, a family is holy not because it is perfect but because God's grace is at work in it, helping it to set out anew every day on the way of love" (p. 11). As long as we can remember to laugh at the oh-so-imperfect way that it sometimes unfolds, we can begin to see glimpses of the holiness that is there in our homes and families—right before our eyes, but usually only evident as we look back and remember.

This notion of the home as the basic unit of the church has underpinned so much of what we have explored in this book, but it may become especially clear when we consider the way we welcome others into our homes. As we mentioned in the section on house blessings at Epiphany, the way that the space and rooms are configured in our homes helps shape what happens there: how and where we gather and how comfortable we feel there. And our days and nights, symbolized by the clocks and calendars we find upon the walls, are the times in which we discover God's presence in many daily ways.

The cleaning, laundry, and cooking that happen daily are holy and important actions, ways that we care for those who live there or those who come to visit. As we mentioned when considering the Eucharist, sharing a meal, whether with guests or just family members, is an especially holy time in our home, although its holiness is usually well disguised with the usual chaos and routine. Our kitchens, for example, are not only very holy places, but also very busy ones. The process of cooking, even with convenience foods undreamt of in the past, still takes a lot of our time and energy.

Brother Lawrence, a cook in a seventeenth-century monastery, had an interesting approach to staying focused on God while being busy about his many tasks: he kept reminding himself that, no matter what he was doing or where he was, God was always present with him. As he would put it, "The time of action does not differ from that of prayer. I possess God as peacefully in the bustle of my kitchen, where sometimes several people are asking me for different things at the same time, as I do upon my knees before the Holy Sacrament" (p. 84). Brother Lawrence would hardly recognize our kitchens because of the machines and conveniences we now enjoy, but his ability to focus on God's presence everywhere is something we can try to achieve as we go about tasks that are both holy *and* ordinary in our homes.

Some families—and some cultures—clearly have more awareness than others of the holiness of hospitality, but whenever we entertain others, God is present in a special way. The author of the letter to the Hebrews reminds his early Christian readers of this important aspect of the domestic church: "Do not neglect hospitality, for through it some have unknowingly entertained angels" (Hebrews 13:2).

MOTHERS AND WORK:
TOO LITTLE TIME

Whether entertaining guests or just caring for their own families, *all* mothers are working mothers, whether or not they work outside the home. Brian Doyle, a father of three and a delightful writer, decided to observe and chronicle what his wife, Mary, did on a single Saturday. He explains:

> I took notes on her labors during a Saturday, on which she punched in at seven in the morning and punched out at midnight. Here is what she did for seventeen hours: baked (bread), bathed (self, progeny), bought (foodstuffs), brushed (cascading hair of self, daughter), carried (sons, bags), changed (diapers, beds), cleaned, combed, consoled (sons, daughter), cooked, danced (with sons), dressed (sons), dried, drove, dug, fed, folded (arms, laundry), hauled, ironed, laughed, mopped (face, floor), mowed, nailed, painted, planted, prayed, pruned (hair, rosebushes), pushed (stroller), read (aloud to daughter), repaired, returned (bottles, plastics), roasted, rocked, sang, scrubbed (sons), shouted, shoveled, swept, swung (sons into bed), talked, taught, washed (dishes, windows), weeded, and wiped (sons, counters, tables.)
>
> What to call this work? Housework seems thin, women's work seems false and insulting, wife's work ditto. I think maybe I will just call it extraordinary and stop there. It is the work of love.

In addition to plenty of work at home—more than we usually realize without an outside observer—today mothers can choose whether or not to work outside the home, a luxury many of our foremothers didn't have.

However, most mothers feel at least some social pressure here, no matter what their choice and the reasons for it. If they are working outside the home, they often feel a need to explain why they aren't home full time with their young children; on the other hand, those who *are* home full time often feel the need to explain why they aren't doing something more to help the family income! (Single parents don't have the luxury of staying home, of course, and currently over 70 percent of mothers with children under eighteen are employed outside the home.)

The issue of juggling work outside and within the home may seem to be a new one for mothers to deal with in the past couple generations, but a further look back will show that—whether in nineteenth-century factories, as slaves, or on the farm—women have often worked outside the home. What may be relatively new about the conversation about mothers and work is both the shape of work today and the way we have isolated mothers from what we consider "work" ever since the Industrial Revolution. For example, most of us have a picture in our heads somewhere of a 1950s-era mom in a TV sitcom doing dishes, a string of pearls around her neck, happy to be home with her children, and waiting for her husband when he comes home—from "work," which involves something for which someone is paid.

Since being a parent is not something for which one is paid, it has become somehow less important in our minds than paid employment—even though we know it's *more* important. Economics writer Ann Crittenden, in her book *The Price of Motherhood: Why the Most Important Job in the World Is Still the Least Valued*, says that women who have children not only are not paid for their work at home but are also penalized financially for caring for children, a "mommy tax" that she calculates at more than a $1 million for a college-educated woman.

The issues of integrating parenting and work don't seem to be as big an issue for men as they are for women, although some writers are now beginning to urge fathers to be more aware of their children in their lives. In fact, in most households where both men and women report that there is an even division of household duties, time studies indicate that mothers are still doing more of the household duties than fathers, a phenomenon that is often referred to as women's "second shift" after they get home from paid employment.

A friend sent this e-mail description of the late part of the second shift. Does this sound familiar?

> Mom and Dad were watching TV when Mom said, "I'm tired, and it's getting late. I think I'll go to bed."
>
> She went to the kitchen to make sandwiches for the next day's lunches, rinsed out the popcorn bowls, took meat out of the freezer for supper the following evening, checked the cereal box levels, filled the sugar container, put spoons and bowls on the table, and started the coffee pot for brewing the next morning.
>
> She, then, put some wet clothes into the dryer, put a load of clothes into the washer, ironed a shirt, and secured a loose button. She picked up the newspapers strewn on the floor, picked up the game pieces left on the table, and put the phonebook back into the drawer. She watered the plants, emptied a wastebasket, and hung up a towel to dry. She yawned and stretched and headed for the bedroom.
>
> She stopped by the desk and wrote a note to the teacher, counted out some cash for the field trip, and pulled a schoolbook out from hiding under a chair. She signed a birthday card for a friend, addressed and stamped the envelope, and wrote a quick list for the grocery store. She put both near her purse. She then washed her face, put on moisturizer, brushed and flossed her teeth.

Hubby called, "I thought you were going to bed." "I'm on my way," she said. She put some water into the dog's dish and put the cat outside, then made sure the doors were locked. She looked in on each of the kids. She turned off a bedside lamp, hung up a shirt, threw some dirty socks in the hamper, and had a brief conversation with the one child who was still awake, doing homework. In her own room, she set the alarm, laid out clothing for the next day, straightened up the shoe rack. She added three things to her list of things to do for tomorrow.

About that time, Hubby turned off the TV and announced, to no one in particular, "I'm going to bed," and . . . he did.

Even without a "second shift," the paid jobs that mothers fill have usually been shaped by a largely male, individualistic, and task orientation; women's values of relationships and family concerns have not influenced our work environments much at all. There are more and more voices calling for flexibility in both work schedules and location to allow for the needs of families—not just mothers—but little is happening so far as a result.

Families also need to look at how they can reshape their duties and expectations at home. In *Also a Mother: Work and Family as Theological Dilemma*, Bonnie Miller-McLemore concludes that one factor that can help relieve some of the pressure on mothers is working toward what she calls a "pitch-in family"—where everybody knows that they have responsibility to help things run well, rather than the "milk and cookies family" where Mom is ultimately responsible for meeting people's needs and making sure things run smoothly. She says this is important not only to help Mom out but also to help everyone to put their Christian love and responsibility for one another into practice. (This will mean, however, that mom may need to revise her standards for some jobs and be willing to ask for help—a tough challenge indeed.)

And then there is the tricky question of childcare when both parents work outside the home. Some couples work separate shifts so that one of them can be home with their children, but that can strongly limit their time as a couple and as a family. Occasionally workers are able to telecommute or work out of their homes. Other families arrange for grandparents or other relatives to watch the children, but most often childcare needs to be arranged with someone outside the family circle. Quality childcare remains a big problem for families everywhere, and the problem won't change much as long as childcare workers continue to be so poorly paid.

Whatever the arrangements for childcare, one of the big concerns for families is getting adequate parent/child contact time. With so many demands on mom's—and everyone's—time, is there enough time for each other? In fact, several recent studies have indicated that mothers working outside the home today may spend up to a half an hour *more* a day with their children than did the stay-at-home mothers of the 1950s and 1960s, who were often cooking and cleaning, as well as socializing with their friends and involved in other non-child-related activities.

As mothers continue to see that what they do *outside their homes* to help make the world a better place is important—as well as what they do in their homes—they will help the emerging process of reflection on the spirituality of work. At its best, the qualities that we bring from our homes to our outside employment and vice versa can be a resource and support to one another, and in both places we are called to help spread Christ's love to a world that so clearly needs it.

Pope John Paul II sounded some important reminders for all of us about this issue in a homily on June 7, 1979:

Motherhood must be treated in work policy and economy as a great end and a great task in itself. For with it is connected the mother's work in giving birth, feeding, and rearing, and no one can take her place. . . . True respect for work brings with it due esteem for motherhood. It cannot be otherwise. The moral health of the whole of society depends on that.

MARRIAGE AND HOLY ORDERS: SACRAMENTS OF COMMITMENT AND SERVICE

When mothers, whether at home or at another job, are caring for others, they are embodying both the commitment and the service that are celebrated in the sacraments of Matrimony and Holy Orders.

Marriage is the only one of the sacraments in which a priest, deacon, or bishop is not the minister; Catholic theology teaches that the couple are ministers of the sacrament *to one another*, because the consent they give to each other in their vows is the key moment in the whole wedding—the visible sign of God's invisible love. Not only can no one else promise the rest of their lives for the bride or groom, but in the wedding vows they are also promising to one another a future that they do not know and cannot foresee.

In the sacrament of marriage they can make this promise forever only because of God's unending love for all of us, which is always there, no matter what. The covenant of their married love—for better and for worse—is based on God's covenant of love for us. And their love is a sign—a sacrament—of God's love in at least three ways: *to each other*, day in and day out, *to others* around them in many ways they don't realize, and *because of the many others* in their lives who have helped them grow and learn to love and who will continue to support them through the years. This bond of love between the spouses also helps mothers to then be a faithful presence of love for their children.

Unfortunately, we are all too aware these days that many marriages *don't* end up lasting forever, even though they intended that on the wedding day. When a decree of nullity—an annulment—is granted in the Catholic Church, after a civil divorce has been obtained, that indicates that some key component was always lacking, making that marriage invalid despite appearances to the contrary.

Just as a couple doesn't know where their promise of forever will take them, as mothers we also take on a commitment to a child without fully knowing where that will lead us. Will this child be famous, be a criminal, or have special needs that will require our attention far more than most children? We don't know what lies ahead with this child or these children, and it's probably just as well. The days, weeks, months, and years unfold in marriage and in parenting, and we are asked to be faithful, not only to the *old* promise we made but also to the *new* promise in the relationship with one another and to finding Christ in the midst of those challenges.

The sacrament of Holy Orders gives us some clues as to what it is that we as mothers are called to *do* in these relationships—even though women are not allowed to be ordained in the Catholic tradition.

Jesus called others to follow him, and after his death the early Christian community needed to find ways to continue his ministry and to designate leaders who could help that happen. They were often chosen through a process of prayer and then blessed through the laying on of hands. Gradually, there emerged within the community the roles of overseer (later called a "bishop"), presbyter (originally a helper and advisor to the bishop, but later a priest), and deacon. (Scholars tell us that there seems to be clear evidence that women were chosen, at least as deacons, in the early centuries of the church.)

Through the centuries there were many changes and developments in ministry, including the development of a number of minor orders, which were revised by the Second Vatican Council in the 1960s. Besides restoring the permanent order of deacon, Vatican II also emphasized the call of *all* Christians through Baptism to follow Christ as a priestly people.

While those who are ordained have special responsibilities, we are all called to serve one another as Jesus did, to use our gifts to help build up the kingdom or reign of God. We each have a unique opportunity to be the presence of Christ in the midst of whatever we are doing as a priestly people, as visible signs of God's invisible love. And mothers are called to serve others in a unique way—day in and day out to teach, preach, and bless in our own way.

MOTHERS SPEAK

Again we hear from mothers and their experience as it relates to the themes of this season of Ordinary Time:

My mother was the mother who did it all. She was the PTA president, she was the camp counselor, the troop leader, the religious education teacher, the neighborhood nurse, and a friend to many in trouble. She was my greatest fan. She never missed a volleyball, basketball, or soccer game—for six years running. She never missed a class field trip or a school event. In high school, she was the "mom" to many of my friends. Our house was a standard stop before most prom or homecoming events. . . . I aspire to be to my children the kind of mother she was to me. And even though my relationship with my children is necessarily different because of my full-time career, I carry many experiences of how to be mother to my children.

Being a mother has turned my life upside down. In the down/rough times my faith was really tried. I really felt like the Lord had abandoned me. My spirituality/prayer life had to really readjust. No longer could I have an hour of quiet time or do extensive journaling as before. I had to learn to pray in the moment and take advantage of little windows of time. My life and motherhood became my prayer. I became a *lot* more flexible, open, able to adapt to various situations. My level of compassion for others has grown tremendously, especially for moms. My child has not been the perfect child; he's been a strong-willed challenge. I've been embarrassed plenty. Being a mom has kept me humble and shown me that God is God and I am not!

I feel intense gratitude when I see my child sleeping at night—gratitude toward God for allowing him into my life and entrusting me with such a fine and precious gift—and gratitude that he's safe at the end of the day—safe to sleep and to dream, rest, and rejuvenate. And I am proud that I just might have something to do with his well-being.

But I also feel an intense anger and almost rage toward my child when we're engaged in a power struggle, when he's noncompliant and argumentative, ESPECIALLY when I'm exhausted and depleted, feeling I have nothing left to give, and/or we are in public. At those times I realize he's got a will independent of mine and he can *choose* to cooperate and work with me . . . or not! There are times when I realize that I don't have the power to make him do what I want, especially when it's imperative, like leaving for work on time, or avoiding the stares in the restaurant when he's screaming because I didn't understand *just* how to cut his blueberry waffle, or when he declares in the middle of my best friend's wedding, "This is boring; I want to go home now," or when he simply won't go to sleep. Then I experience immediate guilt for having such negative and uncomfortable feelings toward the very being for whom I'm also so intensely grateful.

Being a mother is the most difficult and important thing I have ever done. The job is never done. . . . Before kids I was moving right up the corporate ladder. I had a great career in publishing/advertising. I thought I was doing important stuff! I loved my job, and hope to get back to it some day, but right now I am where I am supposed to be. I do miss the paycheck—you don't get those when you're a mom—and the days off—even the coffee breaks were nice. The hardest part for me is that people think that because you are a stay-at-home mom, you must not know how to do anything else. They think the job I left was flipping burgers at the local fast food joint. That boils my blood!

Being a mother is like a tennis match. On one side of the net is this incredible joy and wonder of watching my child learn and develop who he is. On the other side is this incredible guilt that he spends six to seven hours at day care because I really have no choice but to work. This is also mixed with jealousy that the day care people get to spend so much time with my son. And I go back and forth. I know if I stayed home all the time I would go crazy and would be a lousy parent. I also know that we need the income just to provide basic needs for our son.

I have chosen to work half-time to be home with my daughter, and I wouldn't change that decision. It has been great!

My job-share partner is great; she is a support and a friend, and my time with my daughter is wonderful.

My career has always demanded a certain amount of travel. My first travel experience "post" my first child was when he was eight months old. The extreme sadness I felt in leaving him was overwhelming. What kind of mother was I to leave my child? Was this career worth it? How will this be good for him? Since that "first" time, I have traveled over a million miles on many trips away from home. And every time I leave, I have feelings of anxiety about leaving my children. . . . Each time I worry about never seeing them again, about what I will miss when I am gone. But the grace of leaving is that I get to come home and reunite with my children. Every time I return from business travel, I get to appreciate the gift of my children, again and again! Sometimes there are surprises for the kids or even for mom when she gets home. Sometimes, it's just a kiss and a bedtime blessing for a sleeping child. But each time we reunite, for just that first moment, they look changed, older, and have that spark of excitement that says, "Mom, I love you." That's pretty powerful for me.

I went from full time to part time after the birth of my child and have continued at part time for seven years. While my part-time status has kept me from advancing in my career as quickly as I would have on a full-time career track, I have been very fortunate. I'm at the office only when my son is in school or when my husband is home with him. My family is my top priority, and I'm blessed to have an employer that allows me to have flexibility while being highly productive.

In my situation, I have been fortunate to have had the financial means to support a private nanny for my two children, who are eleven and nine. This was a decision my husband and I made when I began pursuing my professional career. It wasn't easy at first; most of my income was used to pay for the nanny. But if I could not be at home to care for our children, I wanted the best possible solution for in-home care. You may ask, "Why not other family members?" With a very large extended family, this was an option for me. However, I consciously decided that I wanted "grandmas to be grandmas." I believe that has enriched the bonds of my children with their grandparents and great-grandparents.

As a working mother, I am a role model, for my children, of how one can be both parent and professional. I hope and pray that my children will not fear the challenge of having both a career and a family, that this will be embraced as possible. Through showing them how to "live" in the midst of exhausting travel schedules and late nights at the office, I hope they will be able to worry less about the impact on their families and their children.

MODELS FROM THE TRADITION

When we look to the saints and others for models of living motherhood day to day and integrating emotions in mothers' spirituality, three examples that emerge are St. Brigid of Ireland, St. Teresa of Avila, and St. Elizabeth Ann Seton.

St. Brigid of Ireland (c. 450–525) eventually became the abbess of Kildare, a double monastery of both men and women. Most of the stories about her have a legendary quality so that it's hard to separate what we would call fact from a magical quality, but there is a clear maternal tone to her generosity. For example, "Once a leprous woman asking for milk, there being none at hand she gave her cold water, but the water was turned into milk, and when she had drunk it the woman was healed" (quoted in Ellsberg, *All Saints*, p. 57). She would often talk the trees into giving their fruit to give away to the poor or the cows to give milk when they should have had none left.

The qualities of hospitality and generosity, so common in mothers, are clearly evident in Brigid. Mothers are often finding situations where some practical help is needed and jumping in to help without a second thought. Whether it's a new neighbor or someone with a new child or someone whose car is not working, a mother is usually there to help.

St. Teresa of Avila (1515–1582) led the reform of her Carmelite religious order after experiencing her own conversion at the age of thirty-nine. Despite considerable opposition and harassment at times from the Spanish Inquisition, she managed to help renew religious life and found seventeen new convents, as well as leave us some key writings about prayer and the religious life. Her deep love of God comes through in these writings, as well as her sense of humor and her willingness to brave all kinds of challenges to her reforms.

"A particular mortification was the misery and hazards of travel at a time when donkey carts were the standard mode of transportation. One time her cart overturned, throwing her into a muddy river. When she complained to God about this ordeal, she heard a voice from within her say, 'This is how I treat my friends.' 'Yes, my Lord,' she answered, 'and that is why you have so few of them'" (Ellsberg, p. 450).

Teresa of Avila helps remind us of the primacy of prayer in mothers' lives, a prayer that doesn't need any formality, but is rather a matter of deep intimacy in the midst of our busy lives.

St. Elizabeth Ann Seton (1774–1821), from a prominent family in early New York, found herself a widow with five young children at the age of twenty-eight, after her husband's business collapsed and his health failed. She had gone to Italy with him for his health, but he died there. Through friends in Italy she became attracted to Catholicism, to which she converted when she returned to the United States, a step that was not supported by her family or her in-laws.

Because of anti-Catholic prejudice she finally moved to Baltimore, where she could begin to provide for her children and others like them the Catholic education they needed. As other women joined to help her, she was also able to live out her dream of starting a religious order for women.

Seton shows us the practical leadership and clear organizational abilities, as well as care of the poor and a focus on the education of children that many mothers possess. In providing what they know their children need, they often end up creating what is also good for the wider community.

Scripture for Reflection

As we reflect on our own day-to-day lives as mothers, the integration of our emotions, and the importance of hospitality to our spirituality, the following passages may be helpful. Please try to take some time with one or more of these passages and with the questions following them. You may prefer to reflect on these with other mothers.

Now as they went on their way, [Jesus] entered a certain village, where a woman named Martha welcomed him into her home. She had a sister named Mary, who sat at the Lord's feet and listened to what he was saying.

But Martha was distracted by her many tasks; so she came to him and asked, "Lord, do you not care that my sister has left me to do all the work by myself? Tell her then to help me." But the Lord answered her, "Martha, Martha, you are worried and distracted by many things; there is need of only one thing. Mary has chosen the better part, which will not be taken away from her." (Luke 10:38-42)

—*With whose "choice" do you identify with most in this passage about hospitality? Why?*
—*Jesus doesn't chide Martha for her choice as much as for comparing herself with her sister. What would he say to you?*

One of the Pharisees asked Jesus to eat with him, and he went into the Pharisee's house and took his place at the table. And a woman in the city, who was a sinner, having learned that he was eating in the Pharisee's house, brought an alabaster jar of ointment. She stood behind him at his feet, weeping, and began to bathe his feet with her tears and to dry them with her hair. Then she continued kissing his feet and anointing them with the ointment. Now when the Pharisee who had invited him saw it, he said to himself, "If this man were a prophet, he would have known who and what kind of woman this is who is touching him—that she is a sinner." Jesus spoke up and said to him, "Simon, I have something to say to you." "Teacher," he replied, "speak." "A certain creditor had two debtors; one owed five hundred denarii, and the other fifty. When they could not pay, he canceled the debts for both of them. Now which of them will love him more?" Simon answered, "I suppose the one for whom he canceled the greater debt." And Jesus said to him, "You have judged rightly." Then turning toward the woman, he said to Simon, "Do you see this woman? I entered your house; you gave me no water for my feet, but she has bathed my feet with her tears and dried them with her hair. You gave me no kiss, but from the time I came in she has not stopped kissing my feet. You did not anoint my head with oil, but she has anointed my feet with ointment. Therefore, I tell you, her sins, which were many, have been forgiven; hence she has shown great love. But the one to whom little is forgiven, loves little." Then he said to her, "Your sins are forgiven."

But those who were at the table with him began to say among themselves, "Who is this who even forgives sins?" And he said to the woman, "Your faith has saved you; go in peace." (Luke 7:36–50)

——*What sights, sounds, and smells do you sense in this rich scene?*
——*How are your emotions part of your prayer?*
——*Most men, especially in Jesus' time, would have been embarrassed in this situation. When you ask Jesus why he wasn't, what does he say in response?*

Now on that same day two of them were going to a village called Emmaus, about seven miles from Jerusalem, and talking with each other about all these things that had happened. While they were talking and discussing, Jesus himself came near and went with them, but their eyes were kept from recognizing him. And he said to them, "What are you discussing with each other while you walk along?" They stood still, looking sad.

Then one of them, whose name was Cleopas, answered him, "Are you the only stranger in Jerusalem who does not know the things that have taken place there in these days?" He asked them, "What things?" They replied, "The things about Jesus of Nazareth, who was a prophet mighty in deed and word before God and all the people, and how our chief priests and leaders handed him over to be condemned to death and crucified him.

But we had hoped that he was the one to redeem Israel. Yes, and besides all this, it is now the third day since these things took place. Moreover, some women of our group astounded us. They were at the tomb early this morning, and when they did not find his body there, they came back and told us that they had indeed seen a vision of angels who said that he was alive. Some of those who were with us went to the tomb and found it just as the women had said; but they did not see him."

Then he said to them, "Oh, how foolish you are, and how slow of heart to believe all that the prophets have declared! Was it not necessary that the Messiah should suffer these things and then enter into his glory?"

Then beginning with Moses and all the prophets, he interpreted to them the things about himself in all the scriptures. As they came near the village to which they were going, he walked ahead as if he were going on.

But they urged him strongly, saying, "Stay with us, because it is almost evening and the day is now nearly over." So he went in to stay with them.

When he was at the table with them, he took bread, blessed and broke it, and gave it to them. Then their eyes were opened, and they recognized him; and he vanished from their sight. They said to each other, "Were not our hearts burning within us while he was talking to us on the road, while he was opening the scriptures to us?"

That same hour they got up and returned to Jerusalem; and they found the eleven and their companions gathered together. They were saying, "The Lord has risen indeed, and he has appeared to Simon!"

Then they told what had happened on the road, and how he had been made known to them in the breaking of the bread. (Luke 24:13–35)

—*Imagine what it would be like to invite Jesus to your house. What would you ask him or talk about?*

—*Think of a time when you talked about your disappointments with a friend over coffee or a meal. How was it similar to this event?*

—*Have you ever had an experience when your faith finally made more sense because of a personal experience? What was that like?*

Other Scripture Passages to Explore

John 4:5–39—Jesus helps the Samaritan woman at the well sort out her marital history and satisfy her thirst for truth.

Deuteronomy 6:1–9—The importance of sharing a reverence for God with all those in your household.

Questions for Individual or Group Reflection

What is the best time of the day for you for prayer? What is the best way for you to pray?

Give an example of how thinking and feeling are connected for you as a mother.

What is your favorite story as a mother? Why? What has this story taught you as a mother?

In what ways is it hardest to see your family as a domestic church? In what ways is it easiest?

What is your biggest challenge when it comes to the issue of work and being a mom?

Resources for This Season

The following are some resources related to the themes explored here; full information on these can be found at the end of this book.

Coffey, *God in the Moment*
M. Finley, *The Ten Commandments*
M. and K. Finley, *Building Christian Families*
Hays, *Pray All Ways*
Linn, *Sleeping with Bread*
Miller-McLemore, *Also a Mother*
Brother Lawrence, *The Practice of the Presence of God*
Rupp, *The Cup of Our Life* and *Out of the Ordinary*

Afterword
To the Reader

Much of what we've explored together here has been said—perhaps more clearly—elsewhere. But I hope that what *has* been helpful here are the connections we've explored between our experiences as mothers and the liturgical year. My hope is that reading this book will be a help to your reflection in somewhat the way that it was for me in the writing of it.

My life ended up being woven in with these topics while I was writing, in ways that I could never have predicted or even imagined. For example, when I was writing about letting go, our oldest son was getting married, and when I was writing about the Anointing of the Sick, my mother discovered that she had cancer and began chemotherapy. Proof, perhaps, of God's warped sense of humor.

The process of writing this also ended up illustrating many of the qualities we've explored here; it was clearly *communal*, in the prayer support I had from so many women and in the reflections they shared with me, and it certainly ended up *emotionally integrated* with the rest of what was happening in my life.

There is more to be said about almost everything I've touched on here, but hopefully we have seen that the Catholic Church—which has traditionally referred to itself as a Mother—has much to give to, as well as much to learn and to receive from, mothers of all kinds as we continue to reflect together on our experience and our spirituality.

Hopefully, together we have begun to explore what the mystic Caryll Houselander expresses so well:

> We must grow in wisdom as Christ did, by deepening our understanding of the sacramental life through the very substance of every day—until there is nothing we see or touch that is not charged with wonder for us, though it is something as familiar as bread on the table; and there is nothing that we do, though it be no more than filling a glass with water for a child, which does not sweep the loveliness of God's sacramental plan through our thoughts, like a great wave of grace washing them clean from sin and the sorrow that is inseparable from it. (*A Child in Winter,* pp. 149–150)

ACKNOWLEDGMENTS

In my experience, no book is written fully alone, and this one is certainly no exception. This "pregnancy" began at the invitation of Jeremy Langford, its editor, who has been patient and supportive through its long "gestation." Kass Dotterweich was an important "midwife," and many friends helped out during the "birth," including Maggie Albo; Jolie Monasterio; Fr. Jim Dallen; Chris Weekly, SJ; and the group of women with whom I have gathered monthly for years, as well as many other mothers who shared their reflections here—not to mention my patient husband and family. "Thank you" doesn't begin to express my gratitude for all their help and support.

RESOURCES

FOR FURTHER READING

Brennan, Patrick. *The Way of Forgiveness: How to Heal Life's Hurts and Restore Broken Relationships.* Ann Arbor, Mich.: Servant, 2000.

A helpful resource showing specific steps for forgiving and seeking forgiveness.

Bridges, William. *Transitions: Making Sense of Life's Changes.* New York: Addison-Wesley, 1980.

Clear and helpful guide to dealing with changes in one's life.

Carr, Ann, and Elisabeth Schussler Fiorenza, eds. *Motherhood: Experience, Institution, Theology.* Edinburgh: T&T Clark, 1989.

Chittister, Joan. *The Story of Ruth: Twelve Moments in Every Woman's Life.* Grand Rapids, Mich.: W. B. Eerdmans, 2000.

A beautiful book which explores the spiritual themes in Ruth for women everywhere.

Coffey, Kathy. *Immersed in the Sacred: Discovering the "Small S" Sacraments.* Notre Dame, Ind.: Ave Maria, 2003.

A look at the everyday holy through a mother and poet's eyes.

———. *God in the Moment: Making Every Day a Prayer.* Chicago: Loyola, 1999.

Cuneen, Sally. *Mother Church: What the Experience of Women Is Teaching Her.* Mahwah, N.J.: Paulist, 1991.

A helpful look at many of the themes of women's lives and spirituality.

Ellsberg, Robert. *All Saints: Daily Reflections on Saints, Prophets, and Witnesses for Our Time.* New York: Crossroad, 1997.

A wonderful collection of short profiles of saints and others, known and little known.

Finley, Kathleen. *Our Family Book of Days: A Record through the Years.* Winona, Minn.: St. Mary's, 1997.

A resource for recording and commemorating a family's "holy times," along with other events, which are already listed.

———. *Savoring God: Praying With All Our Senses.* Notre Dame, Ind.: Ave Maria, 2003.

A how-to resource for praying with many daily objects while using all our senses.

Finley, Mitch. *The Ten Commandments: Timeless Challenges for Today.* Liguori, Mo.: Liguori, 2000.

An interesting exploration of God's law and its implications.

———. *The Seven Gifts of the Holy Spirit.* Liguori, Mo.: Liguori, 2001.

A clear description of the gifts—and fruits—of the Holy Spirit.

Finley, Mitch, and Kathy Finley. *Building Christian Families.* San Jose, Calif.: ASJA, 2000. (Distributed by iUniverse.com.)

A look at the practical implications of the family as the domestic church.

Fischer, Kathleen. *Autumn Gospel: Women in the Second Half of Life.* New York: Paulist, 1995.

A powerful look at the spirituality of aging for women.

Goodman, Ellen, and Patricia O'Brien. *I know Just What You Mean: The Power of Friendship in Women's Lives.* New York: Simon and Schuster, 2000.

A helpful exploration of how women support one another, written by two friends.

Grady, Thomas, and Paula Huston, eds. *Signatures of Grace: Catholic Writers on the Sacraments.* New York: Dutton, 2000.

Intriguing essays by contemporary Catholic writers about the power of the sacraments in their experience.

Harris, Maria. *Dance of the Spirit: The Seven Steps of Women's Spirituality.* New York: Bantam, 1989.

A classic that explores some of the themes mentioned here.

Hays, Edward M. *Pray All Ways.* Easton, Kans.: Forest of Peace, 1981.

Hebbelthwaite, Margaret. *Motherhood and God.* London: Geoffrey Chapman, 1984.

A wonderful personal and theological look at motherhood and at God.

Hillensum, Etty. *An Interrupted Life: The Diaries of Etty Hillesum 1941-43.* New York: Pocket Books, 1981.

A young woman's search for God in Amsterdam in the midst of the Nazi occupation.

Houselander, Caryll. *A Child in Winter: Advent, Christmas and Epiphany with Caryll Houselander.* Edited by Thomas Hoffman. Franklin, Wisc.: Sheed and Ward, 2000.

Wonderful meditations for these seasons by a twentieth-century mystic.

Jaworski, Carol. *Praying the Stations with the Women of the World.* Mystic, Conn.: Twenty-Third Publications, 2002.

A booklet designed to be used with a group but which could also be used alone to help recall the ways that women are suffering today.

Jones, Kathleen. *Women Saints: Lives of Faith and Courage.* Maryknoll, N.Y.: Orbis, 1999.

Profiles of an extraordinary variety of forty holy women.

Lamott, Anne. *Operating Instructions: A Journal of My Son's First Year.* New York: Pantheon, 1993.

Delightful reflections from the mother of a newborn.

Lindbergh, Anne Morrow. *Gift from the Sea.* New York: Pantheon, 1955.

One of the best books on mothers' spirituality from a wonderful writer.

Linn, Dennis, et al. *Sleeping with Bread: Holding What Gives You Life.* Mahwah, N.J.: Paulist, 1995.

An excellent way to help everyone reflect on God's presence in our experience.

Linthorst, Ann Tremaine. *Mothering as a Spiritual Journey: Learning to Let God Nurture Your Children and You along with Them.* New York: Crossroad, 1993.

A wise book for mothers.

Miller-McLemore, Bonnie J. *Also a Mother: Work and Family as Theological Dilemma.* Nashville, Tenn.: Abingdon, 1994.

A feminist theologian looks at the issue of mothers and work.

Montagu, Ashley. *Touching: The Human Significance of Skin.* 2d. ed. New York: Harper & Row, 1978.

A fascinating look by an anthropologist at the importance of touch.

Mulford, Philippa Greene. *Keys to Successful Step-Mothering.* Hauppage, N.Y.: Barron's, 1996.

Helpful how-tos for a challenging role.

Nelson, Gertrud Mueller. *To Dance with God: Family Ritual and Community Celebration.* New York: Paulist, 1986.

A truly wise book about prayer and ritual in the home.

Ochs, Carol. *Women and Spirituality.* Totowa, N.J.: Rowman & Allenheld, 1983.

A good exploration of the themes of women's spirituality and experience.

Ruddick, Sara. *Maternal Thinking: Toward a Politics of Peace.* Boston: Beacon, 1995.

A fascinating philosophical examination of the ways mothers think and the implications for our world.

Rupp, Joyce. *Your Sorrow Is My Sorrow: Hope and Strength in Times of Suffering.* New York: Crossroad, 1999.

A helpful resource for praying with Mary in times of suffering.

———. *The Cup of Our Life: A Guide for Spiritual Growth.* Notre Dame, Ind.: Ave Maria, 1997.

————. *Out of the Ordinary: Prayers, Poems and Reflections for Every Season.* Notre Dame, Ind.: Ave Maria, 2000.

Sanna, Ellyn. *Motherhood: A Spiritual Journey.* New York: Paulist, 1997.
Rich reflections for mothers of any age children.

Schoemperlen, Diane. *Our Lady of the Lost and Found: A Novel of Mary, Faith, and Friendship.* New York: Viking, 2001.
An interesting fictional look at Mary today and her heritage.

Schut, Michael, ed. *Food and Faith: Justice, Joy and Daily Bread.* Denver, Colo.: Living the Good News, 2002.
A look from a variety of perspectives at the importance of food, complete with a study guide.

Swan, Laura. *The Forgotten Desert Mothers: Sayings, Lives, and Stories of Early Christian Women.* New York, Paulist, 2001.
Helpful research on the earliest monastic women.

Tickle, Phyllis, and Christine O'Keeffe Lafser. *An Empty Cradle, a Full Heart: Reflections for Mothers and Fathers after Miscarriage, Stillbirth or Infant Death.* Chicago: Loyola, 1998.
Helpful prayers for a difficult occasion.

Vivas, Julie, illustrator. *The Nativity.* San Diego, Calif.: Harcourt Brace Jovanovich, 1988.
A delightful picture book showing a very human nativity setting.

Wright, Wendy. *Sacred Dwelling: A Spirituality of Family Life.* New York: Crossroad, 1989.
A helpful theological look at the domestic church.

Zukerman, Eugenia. *In My Mother's Closet: An Invitation to Remember.* Notre Dame, Ind.: Sorin, 2003.
Remembrances from women who explored their mothers' closets when they were little.

VIDEOS

Mary, the Mother of Jesus. Directed by Kevin Connor. With Christian Bale, Pernilla August, and Geraldine Chaplin. Hallmark Home Entertainment, 2001.

ORGANIZATIONS

Elizabeth Ministry is an international movement designed to support women and their families during the joys, challenges, and sorrows of the childbearing years. Elizabeth Ministry chapters exist in many places in the world, as well as in the United States. www.elizabethministry.com

MADD (Mothers Against Drunk Driving) is a nonprofit organization whose mission is to stop drunk driving, support victims of this violent crime, and prevent underage drinking; they are not a crusade again alcohol consumption. There are now over 600 chapters, and the organization is now international. www.madd.org

MOMS (Ministry of Mothers Sharing) is an outreach ministry developed by the Benedictine Sisters of St. Paul's Monastery in St. Paul, Minnesota. MOMS awakens in women an awareness of their inner sacred self and teaches them new ways to inspire and affirm each other. Mothers meet together in their local parishes to share with and support one another. Through this personal and spiritual growth, women claim their own giftedness and bring these gifts to the Christian community. www.osb.org/spm/moms.html

Project Rachel is the name of the Catholic Church's healing ministry to those who have been involved in abortion. Its name comes from Jeremiah 31:15-7. Project Rachel operates as a network of professional counselors and priests, all trained to provide one-on-one spiritual and psychological care for those who are suffering because of an abortion. Founded in 1984 by Victoria Thorn in Milwaukee, today Project Rachel programs can be found in 140 Catholic dioceses in the United States, as well as in dioceses in other countries. Also, the **National Office of Post-Abortion Reconciliation and Healing** (NOPARH) sponsors a nation-wide referral service for those seeking help after abortion. For a referral contact NOPARH at **800.5WE.CARE**, or access its website at www.marquette.edu/rachel.

ADDITIONAL REFERENCES

St. Augustine of Hippo. *The Confessions.* New York: New City Press, 1997.

American Heritage Dictionary. New York: Houghton Mifflin, 1997.

Chesto, Kathleen. "On the Judgment." *Family-Centered Intergenerational Religious Education.* Sheed and Ward, 1988.

Colledge, Edmund, and James Walsh, eds. *Julian of Norwich: Showings.* Mahwah, NJ: Paulist, 1978.

Crittenden, Ann. *The Price of Motherhood: Why the Most Important Job in the World Is the Least Valued.* New York: Owl Books, 2002.

Curran, Dolores. "This Time It's Personal." *U.S. Catholic,* August 2000.

Dillard, Annie. *Teaching a Stone to Talk.* New York: Harper and Row, 1982.

Doyle, Brian. *Portland Magazine.* Winter 1996.

Fragoumeni, Fr. Richard. *Come to the Feast: An Introduction to Eucharistic Transformation*. New York: Continuum, 1997.

Gordon, Mary. *Men and Angels*. New York: Random House, 1985.

Hendrickson, Mary Lynn. "Weekly Meditations for Busy Parents," a free service of *At Home with Our Faith* newsletter, sponsored by the Claretian Missionaries. Website: www. homefaith.com, phone: 1-800-328-6515.

Hughes and Francis, eds. *Living No Longer for Ourselves: Liturgy and Justice in the Nineties*. Liturgical Press, 1991.

Johnson, Elizabeth. *She Who Is: The Mystery of God in Feminist Theological Discourse*. New York: Crossroad, 1994.

Lawrence, Brother. *The Practice of the Presence of God*. Nashville: Thomas Nelson, 1981.

McBrien, Richard P., ed. *HarperCollins Encyclopedia of Catholicism*. San Francisco, Calif.: HarperSanFrancisco, 1995.

McFague, Sally. *Models of God: Theology for an Ecological, Nuclear Age*. Fortress, 1975.

———. "Mother God," in *Motherhood: Experience, Institution, Theology*, edited by Anne Carr and Elisabeth Schussler Fiorenza. Edinburgh: T&T Clark, 1989.

Ohanneson, Joan. *Woman: Survivor in the Church*. Winston, 1980.

Pope John XXIII. *Journal of a Soul*. New York: Doubleday, 1980.

Prejean, Sister Helen. *Dead Man Walking: An Eyewitness Account of the Death Penalty in the United States*. New York: Vintage, 1994.

U.S. Bishops. *Follow the Way of Love*. Washington, DC: USCCB, 1994.

ABOUT THE AUTHOR

Kathleen Finley is a mother of three young adult sons and is married to Mitch Finley, also a prominent Catholic author. She is a well-known teacher, speaker, and writer on topics of women's, marital, and family spirituality. She currently teaches at Gonzaga University in Spokane, Washington, when she's not working with engaged couples or speaking or writing on practical spirituality for women and families.

to Ann Lowe,
with love and thanks